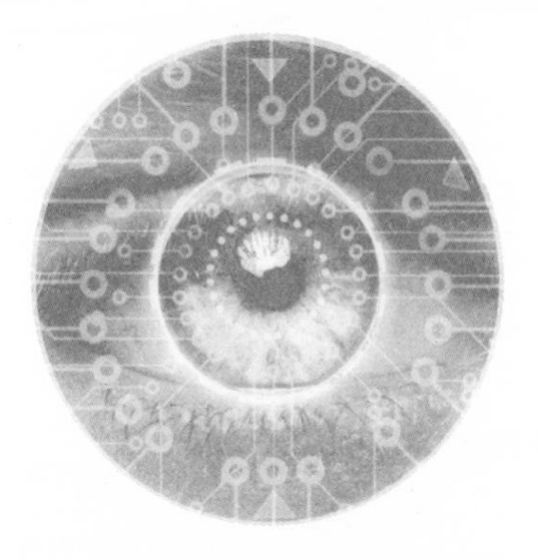

Robots, Ethics and the Future of Jobs

Seán McDonagh

Published by Messenger Publications, 2021

ISBN 978 1 78812 306 8

Designed by Messenger Publications Design Department
Cover Image: © Zapp2Photo / Shutterstock
Typeset in Plantin MT Pro & Bitter
Printed by Hussar Books

Messenger Publications,
37 Leeson Place, Dublin D02 E5V0
www.messenger.ie

For my lifelong friend,
Sister Patricia Greene, RSM
– a woman of great compassion, kindness and
love, whose entire life has been spent in
the service of others.

I love my robot lawn mowers, my laptop, WiFi, Google, Facetime, WhatsApp and the possibility of drone postal deliveries and more. Yet worries nag about being overwhelmed by an AI revolution whose ethical and moral parameters are less clear than its rampant profiteering from and monetising of your lives and mine. This hugely informative book shakes us out of our massage armchairs and demands that we engage immediately with these galloping advances so we can shape them to the benefit of the many and not leave them to the enrichment of the few at the awful cost of the impoverishment of swathes of humanity.

Mary McAleese,
former president of Ireland

Seán McDonagh investigates the impacts of the new fusion of physical, digital and biological technologies – the so-called Fourth Industrial Revolution – on our social and working lives: 'artificial intelligence' in industry, farming, social and healthcare, finance, transport, security, and armed conflict. The positive potentials of these technologies for improving life together on a sustainable planet are not disputed, but the negative and radical effects are just as concrete. Seán McDonagh argues that a universal basic income can offset the undesirable impacts of replacement technologies on workers. This is more than a mere technical shoring-up against a tide of social disturbance. It is part of his life-long commitment to international inequality alleviation and planetary wellbeing, and to Catholic social teaching's emphasis on the dignity of work, on freedom for human creativity, and care for creation.

Professor Cathriona Russell,
School of Religion, TCD.

As we enter the Brave New World where control and automation potentially remove our hard-fought freedoms as well as our jobs, this book asks searching questions of how society should respond ethically to the threats posed. Based on a lifetime of working with the poor and oppressed, and conscious of the risk of environmental destruction, Seán McDonagh provides great insight into the important role to be played by world religions in providing the vital moral compass we need.

Professor John Sweeney
Department of Geography, Maynooth University

Robots, Ethics and The Future of Jobs is a wakeup call for political, civic, media and church leaders, urging a response to the deepening and accelerating pace of technological change and its potential consequences. AI, robotics, drones, the internet of things and 3D printing are the building blocks of the fourth industrial revolution. These technologies offer great potential but also carry real risks and are reaching into every corner of our lives, civilian and military. Who will win and who will lose? Who will set the rules and the ethical boundaries within which they should develop and operate? Will the displaced be included, if so, how; or ignored and, if so, with what political, social and economic consequences? That these questions cannot be avoided and should not be postponed – and that we do not need to wait for change to happen because it is already upon us – are central messages of this thought-provoking text.

Pat Cox,
former president of the European Parliament

Acknowledgements

I would like to thank Elizabeth McArdle and Pauline Connolly for all the assistance they gave me while writing this book. Special thanks to John Fahey and Will Flanagan whose insights and comments on the first draft were very valuable. My colleague and fellow Columban, Diarmuid Healy helped me in so many ways. Cecilia West and Kate Kiernan from Messenger Publications were always most supportive. Finally, I would like to thank my sister, Maire, for reading every draft of the book and meticulously proof-reading the final draft.

Contents

Foreword

In the summer of 2019, I was invited to give a keynote talk at the annual conference of Societas Ethica, the European Society for Research in Ethics, which that year was organised around the theme of 'Digital Humanity: Ethical Analyses and Responses in the Age of Transformation'. The event would consider the individual and societal impact of global digitalisation, and ponder how philosophical and theological ethicists might effectively respond to these challenges. Founded in 1964, Societas Ethica describes itself as 'a platform for the exchange of scholarly work, ideas and experiences stemming from different philosophical and theological traditions'.

After some thought, I accepted, even though I was not a philosopher, much less a theologian. The conference topic intrigued me, and the invitation was unexpected and outside my usual experience. I imagined I would present my talk – on the secretive encroachment of technology, especially the big tech platforms, into our private lives – and then go sightseeing around the lovely Bavarian lakeside setting of the conference. I also hoped a few of the presentations might prove accessible to a non-philosopher/theologian.

As it turned out, I attended nearly every session. The talks were wonderfully thought-provoking. Looking at these issues in what was, for me, a very different context, was both a personally compelling challenge and a revelation. I later wrote in *The Irish Times* about a paper presented by Dr James Caccamo, an associate professor of theology at St Joseph's University in Philadelphia. His essay, entitled '(Morally) Sustainable Employment for the Digitalised Workforce', looked at the 'gig economy' – that emergent economy of freelance and contract workers who provide their labour with few to none of the entitlements or protections of employees – viewed in the context of the Catholic Church's Integral Human Development goals.

I noted that this intriguing paper, and so many others at the conference, had offered me 'a new way of thinking about shared concerns and helped me realise that different approaches can make such topics accessible and compelling to different audiences'.

This is extremely important. We need diverse ethical frameworks and many types of deep thinking, including the theological, to better understand and address the potential repercussions of a digital world that, as Fr Seán McDonagh's *Robots, Ethics and the Future of Jobs* makes clear, comes at us very fast, with little regulation and few guiding policies or protections.

In tackling the subjects of robotics, artificial intelligence (AI) and machine-driven automation, Fr McDonagh takes on some of today's most concerning technologies. Each of these terms is shorthand for multifaceted technology sectors that, as he rightly points out, regularly slip under our collective societal, political and ethical radar.

He notes early on how algorithms – the computing formulas underlying digital technologies – operate with escalating but hidden complexity, while making decisions that affect lives. They often function with the inbuilt, unacknowledged, unseen biases of predominantly young male coders (women, he notes, make up only 22% of the AI workforce). In some cases, we cannot even understand how AI makes decisions, because it can learn and adapt.

In Covid-19-era Ireland, we have seen how a faulty Leaving Certificate grading algorithm can affect the educational plans of thousands of students. With that insight, now (re)consider our algorithm-driven world of autonomous cars and trucks, of weaponised, lethal, remotely-operated drones, of global financial markets in which algorithms conduct a large portion of daily trading, of robotic assistants and teachers in care homes and schools. As the book makes clear, these are existing or pending realities, not remote future scenarios for later generations to grapple with.

One of the helpful strengths of this book is its wide array of examples of these technologies and their real-world applications, explained in an approachable, non-technical way for readers wanting to understand some of their benefits but, also, the ethical dilemmas they present. Always to the forefront is a consideration of how these technologies are likely to alter the world of work, even eliminate swathes of it, and what that might mean for people who may not easily find any replacement employment, whose entire human skillset might have been obliterated by a digital brain.

As Fr McDonagh points out, few politicians, academics or religious leaders, internationally or in Ireland, are thinking about such issues in a comprehensive way, despite the fact that many workers are in the crosshairs of these technologies, from the most vulnerable poor in the developing world to middle class professionals.

Robots, Ethics and the Future of Jobs is an accessible and thoughtful look at these fascinating, yet disturbing technologies, poised to bring societal change on the magnitude of the Industrial Revolution. As Fr McDonagh makes clear, we all need to be thinking about the profound implications of these technologies, and persuading those in power that they cannot continue to be developed and deployed in an ethics-free environment.

Dr Karlin Lillington is a journalist who writes on technology and culture for *The Irish Times* and *The Guardian* and many others publications.

Introduction
Artificial Intelligence (AI) Technologies Have Speeded Up Hugely in the Last Forty Years

Unbelievable strides have been made in both computer and communication technologies during the past forty years. When my father died in the mid-1970s, I promised to telephone my mother every month. At that time, I was working as a missionary among the T'boli, a tribal people in southwest Mindanao, in the Philippines. Due to their location, they had very little contact with the outside world until after the Second World War.

Making a telephone call to Ireland was difficult. It meant a bus journey to Davao City from T'boli town, which was situated in the province of South Cotabato. Davao is the largest city in Mindanao and was the only place on the island that had an international telephone connection at the time. The bus journey could take from four to six hours, depending on the condition of the road and the bus. If one of the tyres was punctured, that could take half an hour or more to fix. On reaching Davao City, I headed for the overseas telephone centre to book the telephone call. Normally, I booked my call for four o'clock in the afternoon, as Philippines time was eight hours ahead of GMT. I usually booked a ten-minute call, but the overseas connection would often break down after four or five minutes and, frequently, could not be restored. Since my community did not have a house in Davao, I stayed the night at the house of the Maryknoll Missionaries, before heading back to T'boli town the following morning. Contrast the effort, drudgery and time which it took to make that call in the 1980s with the speed and ease of telephoning people globally today. For the past number of years it has been possible to phone, text, Skype or email people who are working in Lake Sebu, in T'boli town. Many of these people now have Facebook accounts or use other social media platforms.

My Surprise the First Time I Saw a Mobile Phone

The first time I saw a mobile phone used was during a visit to Hong Kong in the early 1980s. The device looked like a large Bord na Móna turf briquette, and the battery, which was huge, lasted for less than an hour. At that moment, I did not think that this technology would become commonplace and be a central part of global communications technology in the future. If fact, if I had been told then that, within forty years, there would be four billion mobile phones in use on earth, I would have dismissed it as unbelievable. In 2020, more than four billion phones were indeed being used across the globe. Making a global phone call today takes just a few minutes.

Another illustration of this took place in January 1988 when the Catholic bishops of the Philippines became the first episcopal conference in the world to publish a pastoral letter on the care of the earth, *What is Happening to Our Beautiful Land?* I was one of the main drafters of the document and was invited to address the Bishops' Conference at a meeting, in Tagaytay near Manila, in advance of the bishops' approval of the text. Before the meeting my attention was drawn to an incorrect reference cited in the document. I had to take a bus from Tagaytay to the Jesuit university, the Ateneo de Manila, to check the correct reference for the document. That evening, I stayed at the Columban house in Manila, returning to Tagaytay the following morning. Correcting one citation took me a day and a half. If I had had access to the internet at that time, I could have amended the text in two or three minutes.

Of course, my current mobile phone is not just a device that allows me to make calls and send text messages. I can send emails to people all over the world and I can access the internet. I can use my phone to do web banking and it allows me to play games, listen to my favourite music and use a GPS (Global Positioning System) camera. Google Maps helps me to locate addresses across the world. I can also watch all kinds of videos and check for current news items.

AI and Medicine

In 2020, with every country in the world attempting to fight Covid-19, researchers are using AI to understand the coronavirus more thoroughly, to find drugs that can cure it and to create a vaccine. In February 2020, researchers at the London start-up, Benevolent AI, published a letter in the medical journal, *The Lancet*. It described how the company is using machine-learning algorithms to identify a drug that could fight Covid-19.[1] In Thailand, hospitals are deploying 'ninja robots' to measure the fever level of coronavirus patients and to protect the health of medical workers on the frontlines. These robots were first developed to monitor recovering stroke patients. Now, they are being used to fight Covid-19.[2] In April 2020, Apple and Google announced that they would use their sophisticated technology to trace people that may be infected with Covid-19.

While that is very admirable during a pandemic crisis, many would fear that, in the future, the same tools would be used to track migrants or refugees when the pandemic has passed. That is why respect for human rights must be at the heart of all these new technologies, such as drones and facial recognition photography.

In many countries during the Covid-19 lockdown, WhatsApp enabled millions of grandparents and grandchildren to connect with and see each other as they communicated on the phone. On this level, WhatsApp and similar platforms were a great support for

1 Alex Pasternack, 'The technology and medicine we need to fight the coronavirus', Fast Company, 18 March 2020 (https://www.fastcompany.com).
2 RTE News 'Thai hospitals deploy "ninja robots" to aid virus battle', 19 March 2020 (https://www.rte.ie/news/coronavirus/2020/0319/1124068-coronavirus-world/).

families that had to keep apart physically during the pandemic. It is also a wonderful technology for keeping in touch with older people in the community who may not have family living in the area, so that they do not feel cut off or disconnected from the community.

However, there is also a downside to how these technologies are structured and how they are used. As governments and medical personnel attempt to inform people about what is happening with this novel coronavirus, their efforts are being undermined by the spread of misinformation regarding the origin of the virus and false claims regarding cures. On 17 March 2020, Věra Jourová, Vice-President of the European Commission for Values and Transparency, said that 'it is clear ... that a lot of false information continues to appear in the public sphere. In particular, we need to understand better the risks related to communication on end-to-end encryption services.'[3]

These technologies can be very beneficial, so we should be grateful for the breakthroughs in vital information. However, the new technologies, and the corporations that control them, such as Facebook, Amazon, Microsoft and Google, can have a serious negative impact on our privacy and our freedom. This has been outlined by Shoshana Zuboff in her book, *The Age of Surveillance Capitalism: The Fight for a Human Future at the New Frontier of Power.*[4] The book points out that these companies use people's data including, for example, their facial expressions, to analyse their emotions. The amount of data these companies amass on an individual is astonishing, and the algorithms that they use to process it are so all-encompassing that they can assure their customers that their products will be bought more readily. Most of Facebook's revenue comes from advertising and it is a very lucrative business. The same is true for the tech companies. Surveillance capitalism has made these companies very rich over the last twenty years.

3 Hadas Gold and Donie O'Sullivan, 'Facebook has a coronavirus problem. It's WhatsApp', CNN, 19 March 2020.

4 Shoshana Zuboff, *The Age of Surveillance Capitalism: The Fight for a Human Future at the New Frontier of Power,* London: Profile Books, 2019.

Zuboff argues that surveillance misuses our privacy and undermines our freedom, and, therefore, it should be opposed through comprehensive regulations. She also argues that email users, for example, who think that the service is both convenient and free, are unaware that the goal of such companies is to develop predictive data, which they sell to advertisers for large amounts of money.

A study completed in 2018 showed that about 40 per cent of EU citizens have been targeted by advertisements that are a response to sensitive information about their sexuality, religion or politics. The study was conducted by Ángel Cuevas Rumín and colleagues based in Charles III University of Madrid.[5] Before Cuevas began the study, he browsed through Facebook and saw an advertisement inviting him to connect with a gay group. Though he had never given Facebook any information about his sexuality, Facebook had categorised him as having same-sex tendencies. To show how easy it is to target people based on sensitive information they may have supplied, Cuevas's team purchased three Facebook advertisement campaigns. One group targeted users interested in religion. Another targeted users based on their political opinions, and the last group was based on those who were interested in homosexuality. For €25, the three groups were able to reach more than 25,000 people. In response to a *New Scientist* query, Facebook claimed that their advertising is fully compliant with current Irish data protection legislation. *New Scientist* contacted independent data protection experts and expressed concern about personal data being used in this way.

In reviewing Zuboff's book, Fintan O'Toole of *The Irish Times* writes that it 'quite possibly the single most important book about politics, economics, culture and society in this century. She explains with far more power than anyone has done before the emergence

5 Timothy Revell, 'What's not to like?' *New Scientist*, 24 February 2018.

of a whole new form of capitalism based on the expropriation of personal data we freely give to vast corporations.'[6] These companies know a lot about a person's behaviour through their use of the internet, apps and smart appliances. We, on the other hand, know very little about the companies and how they use our data and monetise it. And, that is the way these companies would like the situation to remain.

Zuboff points out that before the 9/11 attack, the US government was in the process of developing serious regulations to give web users real choices about how their personal information was stored and used. According to her, 'in a few days the concern shifted from "How do we regulate these companies that are violating privacy norms and rights?" to "How do we regulate and protect these companies as they collect data for us?"'[7]

There are also problems with other platforms. When a person uses Google to search the internet, it keeps their search history forever. This means that Google knows every search we have ever made over the years. It also tracks every video we watch on YouTube and other platforms. Even if we do not use Google products regularly, the company can still discover a lot about us – Google trackers have been found on 75 per cent of the million most popularly viewed websites. Those who use Google Home may not know that the device records every live command by the user or anyone else in the house. When we email, Google stores all our emails and contacts. Using Google location services, it also tracks every place we have been. The reason Google wants to know so much about us is to promote their advertising revenue. With all these strategies, Google builds a robust, accurate profile about a person because they know that advertisers prefer to buy ads that are targeted to specific people and their needs. In fact, it would be more accurate to look on Google as a tracking company. It records each time we see advertisements

6 Shoshana Zuboff, op. cit.
7 Peter C. Barker, 'We can't go back to normal: how will coronavirus change the world?' *The Guardian*, 30 March 2020.

and, more importantly, whether or not we click on them.

Zuboff is convinced that surveillance capitalism will affect society at large, as privacy is essential to the functioning of democratic institutions such as voting, dealing with the police, the court system and banking. According to Zuboff, 'many hopes today are pinned on the new body of EU regulations known as the General Data Protection Regulations (GDPR), which became enforceable in May 2018. The EU approach differs fundamentally from that of the US in that companies must justify their data activities within the GDPR regulatory framework.'[8] We will see in Chapter 2 that the GDPR regulations are not working as well as they should because of lack of funding and trained personnel.

In Ireland, since February 2020, 'big tech' companies are being investigated by the Data Protection Commissioner. In Facebook's case, the regulator is investigating three alleged breaches of GDPR. In addition, the regulator is also investigating the lawful basis on which the company processes the personal data of Facebook users. In the case of WhatsApp and Instagram, the regulator is investigating the processing of personal data and the transparency of the information that is given to its users.[9] These are just two examples, but this battle against the intrusive and unlawful activities of tech companies must continue if we are to extricate ourselves from their clutches. In fact, this is one of the major justice issues of our time.

On 16 July 2020, the EU Court of Justice ruled that in the long battle between Facebook, Ireland's Data Protection (DPC) and Max Schrems, an Austrian privacy activist, the so-called Privacy Shield agreement does not offer adequate protection for EU citizens' personal data. Writing in *The Irish Times,* Naomi O'Leary said that 'the ruling is a blow to the thousands of companies, including Facebook, that rely on the Privacy Shield to transfer data across the Atlantic, and to the European Commission, as it unpicks the

8 Ibid., 481.

9 Simon Carswell, 'Which big companies are being investigated by the data regulator?' *The Irish Times,* 20 February 2020.

arrangement it designed with US authorities to allow companies to comply with EU data protection law.'[10]

Many journalists and publishers applauded the Australian government's decision to force large tech giants such as Google and Facebook to pay media outlets for news content published on their platforms. News content has been very profitable for large online platforms. In 2018, Google made a profit of $4.7 billion dollars from content produced by other news companies. Google challenges the accuracy of those figures, but other news media organisations and governments are concerned about the impact Google is having on the news industry, where many journalists are losing their jobs and publications are closing down.

On 20 October 2020, the US Justice Department filed a lawsuit against Google, which is a unit of Alphabet in Washington DC The Department accused the company of maintaining an illegal monopoly over search and search advertising. The Department argues that these exclusionary practices are harmful to competition and undermine innovation in the technology sector. It seems that seven states are also considering their own antitrust suits against Google.[11]

On another front, Australian Treasurer Josh Frydenberg told the Australian Broadcasting Corporation in April 2020 that 'we can't deny the importance of creating a level playing field, ensuring a fair go for companies and the appropriate compensation for content'. Frydenberg recognises that this is a very serious issue, and also that he is dealing with very powerful corporations. A report from the Australian Competition and Consumer Commission states that for every $100 spent on online advertising, AU$47 goes to Google, AU$24 goes to Facebook and a pittance of only AU$29 is left for everyone else.[12] Frydenberg went on to say that 'We

10 Naomi O'Leary, 'EU's top court rules Privacy Shield data agreement invalid', *The Irish Times*, 17 July 2020.

11 Kang, McCabe, and Wakabayashi, 'U.S. Accuses Google of Illegally Protecting Monopoly', *The New York Times*, 20 October 2020.

12 Digital Platforms Inquiry – Final Report', ACCC, June 2019, p.126.

won't bow to their threats. This is a big mountain to climb. These are big companies that we're dealing with, but there's so much at stake that we are prepared to fight.'[13] Australian journalists hope that their government will lead the way with strict enforcement. Monica Attard, head of journalism at the University of Technology in Sydney, hopes that the Australian government's decision could lay the foundation for other governments around the world to 'go after the big giants'.[14]

Reflecting on the decision of the Australian government to force big tech companies to pay other companies for media content, Karlin Lillington, writing in *The Irish Times* in April 2020, made the point that Google and Facebook now control around 60 per cent of the global advertising market and that the journalists and media groups who research and report on daily events, both locally and globally, get only a pittance of the advertising revenue. As a result, newspapers reporting on these events are decreasing and media companies are closing down. With competent journalism under threat, this immediately gives way to the world of fake news and conspiracy theories. Lillington and many others believe that gathering our personal data should be banned.[15]

On 25 April 2020, the then Irish Taoiseach Leo Varadkar, while acknowledging that Google, Facebook and Twitter are great companies, said that 'they are free riders on costs incurred by other people'. He went on to say that 'the Australian approach is innovative and interesting'.[16] Varadkar believes that the next government will consider methods to oblige tech companies to share advertisements 'more fairly' with other news and content producers. In 2019,

13 Livia Albeck-Ripka, 'Australia Moves to Force Google and Facebook to Compensate Media Outlets', *The New York Times*, 20 April 2020 (https://www.nytimes.com/2020/04/20/business/media/australia-facebook-google.html).

14 Ibid.

15 Karlin Lillington, 'It's time to ban websites from gathering our personal data', *The Irish Times*, 23 April 2020 (https://www.irishtimes.com/business/technology/it-s-time-to-ban-websites-from-gathering-our-personal-data-1.4235357).

16 Fiach Kelly, 'Tech giants "free riders" on media content – Varadkar', *The Irish Times*, 25 April 2020.

marketing group Core estimated that between them Google and Facebook collected 40 per cent of total advertising in the Irish Republic, which is why legislation is needed to protect traditional media.[17]

Ethics and AI

Ethics must play a key role in developing a code of conduct for the software industry. The Catholic Church is very interested in software ethics and the various aspects of our lives that are influenced by software. The Pontifical Academy for Life ran a two-day conference, from 28–29 February 2020, on the ethical use of AI technology. The conference promoted what they called 'algor-ethics', which is the ethical use of AI 'according to the principles of transparency, inclusion, responsibility, impartiality, reliability, security and privacy.'[18] Pope Francis was scheduled to speak at the conference, but had to cancel because he was unwell. The Pope's paper was read by Archbishop Vincenzo Paglia, the president of the Academy for Life. The Pope was clear that 'the aim of the ethical development of algorithms is to ensure a review of the 'processes by which we integrate relationships between human beings and today's technology'.[19] The Pope continued that 'the Church's social teaching on the dignity of the person, justice, subsidiarity and solidarity is a critical contribution in the pursuit of these goals'.[20] Beyond that, he admitted that the complexity of the technological world demands of us an increasingly clear ethical framework so as to make this commitment truly effective. In his encyclical, *Fratelli Tutti* (On Fraternity and Social Friendship), which was published in October 2020, Pope Francis is very critical of how the digital culture is being used to stir up campaigns of hatred and destruction (*FT*,

17 Laura Slattery, 'Is this the moment of truth for Facebook and Google?', *The Irish Times*, 25 April 2020.
18 'Hannah Brockhaus, 'Pontifical Academy for Life, tech companies, call for ethical use of AI technology', Catholic News Agency, 28 February 2020.
19 Ibid.
20 Ibid.

43). He focuses on the constant and febrile bonding that encourages hostility, insults and abuse of others without the restraints which normally would occur when people are in each other's presence. This type of 'social aggression has found unparalleled room for expansion through computers and mobile devices.'[21]

We must ensure that ethical considerations are factored in at every stage of the development of these technologies. A Washington University law professor, Ryan Calo, has called for the development of a Federal Robotics Commission in the US, which would monitor and regulate developments in AI so that they do not encourage irresponsible use of these technologies. Calo argues that if you create entities that think for themselves and can make choices, serious theological questions will arise, which religions must address.[22]

Governments, parliaments and international bodies have an important role to play in preventing criminal groups or rogue states using cybertechnology and machine learning for destructive purposes. In 2020, at the time of writing, tech companies regulate themselves. Companies such as Google have formed ethics boards to help monitor their own activities in the area of machine learning and AI. However, having companies monitor their own behaviour is very unsatisfactory, as we learned in relation to banks during the financial crash of 2008.

Companies can also put pressure on large tech giants to act more responsibly. In June 2020, Facebook came under pressure for failing to take down a post by President Donald Trump that stated 'When the looting starts, the shooting starts.'[23] The President was referring to the protest against police brutality following the killing of George Floyd. Because of Facebook's unwillingness to take down this hate speech, a growing number of leading companies

21 Pope Francis, *Fratelli Tutti, On Fraternity and Social Friendship,* Vatican City, 4 October 2020, Par. 44.

22 Jonathan Merritt, 'Is AI a Threat to Christianity? Are you there, God? It's a robot', *The Atlantic*, 3 February 2017 (https://www,theatlantic.com/archives/2017/02/artificial-intelligence-chrisitanity/515463).

23 Hannah Murphy, 'Unilever pulls US ads from Facebook and Twitter over hate speech concerns', *Financial Times*, 27 June 2020.

decided to boycott Facebook. These include Verizon, Unilever, Coca-Cola, Diageo, Honda America, Levi Strauss and Company, Patagonia and Starbucks. According to the ad intelligence group Pathmatics, Verizon spent an estimated $850,000 on advertising on Facebook during the first three weeks of June 2020, while Unilever spent $500,000 over the same period. Almost immediately Mark Zuckerberg responded and announced a series of measures and new policies, including a ban on hateful content directed towards immigrants and African-Americans. Those who have organised the boycott hope that worldwide action can motivate Facebook to be much more proactive in eliminating hate speech in the future.

Moore's Law

This computing term, which originated in the 1970s, stipulates that the processing power of computers doubles every two or three years, and this is why computers are becoming more powerful. The doubling effect of these technologies is increasing significantly. Satya Nadella, CEO of Microsoft, stated in April 2020 that, because the coronavirus had caused people to spend more time online, the software giant had seen 'two years' worth of digital transformations [accomplished] in two months.'[24] It is clear that in the post-Covid-19 era, we are not going back to the past, in fact, this is the new normal.

In Chapter 1, I point out that AI, robots and drones have benefited, and will continue to benefit, our society in many ways. The downside of this is that it may be impossible for 40–50 per cent of people worldwide to find paid employment.

Chapter 2 will focus on AI and will highlight the rapid development of algorithms. AI offers us very powerful tools which, for good or ill, will shape debates in our society for decades to come. It will examine how well institutions such as the Data Protection Commission are helping us to cope with the broad reach of surveillance capitalism.

24 Gaby Hinsliff, 'New technology tends to be difficult to implement. Unfortunately for many workers, difficult is the new normal', *The Guardian*, 30 April 2020.

Chapter 3 discusses how 3D printing is transforming manufacturing, the building industry and medical technologies. These areas of the economy have created a significant number of jobs for workers during the last hundred years or more. 3D printing could have major implications for developing countries' economies because, in the future, developed countries may not outsource the manufacturing of their goods. With 3D capability, developed countries will manufacture their goods locally. This will have a catastrophic impact on developing economies, such as those of Bangladesh and Indonesia.

Chapter 4 explains how the recent development of robots and drones has had a massive impact on many aspects of our society. Drones and robots are used in the retail trade, in education, in the building industry and in mining. I will argue that this will have a huge negative impact on jobs in the future.

Chapter 5 will focus on the use of robots in agriculture. Dr Peter Mooney is a senior researcher at the Department of Computer Science at Maynooth University, Ireland. He believes that running a smart farm in the future will involve getting more value out of agriculture through information technology, mobile phones, apps and the internet in general. Once again, as these technologies begin to be used on an increasing number of farms, they will have an adverse impact on migrant workers.

Chapter 6 will deal with how adopting these new technologies will affect people who work in nursing homes, those caring for sick and the elderly and, also, those who work with young people.

Chapter 7 will consider the economic sector and look at how new technologies will impact on the retail trade, banking, investment, insurance and accountancy. Many people have worked in these professions in the past, but now there will be a haemorrhaging of jobs as robot stores, robot hotels, investment algorithms and robot accountants take jobs and exclude people.

Chapter 8 shifts the focus to the impact that autonomous cars and trucks will have on society and the economy in the future. In 2018, millions of trucks moved goods around the US, Europe and Asia. According to the American Trucking Association, there are approximately 3.5 million professional truck drivers in the US. A large back-up of hotels, motels and shops services this important sector of the economy. I am predicting that this sector will see major changes in the next twenty years and will employ fewer people.

Chapter 9 looks at the development and impact of military robots and drones on warfare worldwide. Some commentators compare these new developments in military hardware with the creation of atomic and nuclear weapons in the 1940s and 1950s. We know that nuclear weapons cannot be deployed because their use would destroy vast areas of the world for thousands of years. Unfortunately, military robots and drones can be used, not just by governments, but also by terrorists, as drones are relatively inexpensive to manufacture. One thing is certain, military conflicts in the future will not be fought as they were in the past. This chapter deals with the ethics of killer drones and argues that the use of autonomous weapons is immoral.

Chapter 10 makes the case for a universal basic income (UBI) since, in the future, many people will not have a paid job and will not have enough money to meet their basic needs. Unless this problem is addressed we could be creating a very unequal society, with a small group of very wealthy people profiting and the rest of the population living from hand to mouth.

Chapter 11 will examine the new technologies in the light of the key points of Catholic social teaching, particularly the meaningfulness of work and its importance for human beings. If 40–50 per cent of people cannot find jobs, how will we cope? This is an issue that must be confronted now.

Explanation of Terms Used

Some terms in this book may require explanation. I have already mentioned **artificial intelligence** (AI).

In computer science, an **algorithm** is a set of instructions to solve a problem or perform a computation. The term algorithm itself is called after the Persian scholar, Muhammad ibn Mūsā al-Khwārizmī (AD 780–850). He lived in Baghdad under the patronage of Caliph Al-Ma'Mun, and produced works on mathematics and astronomy. Because of his seminal work on linear and quadratic equations, he is also known as the father of algebra. In Latin, he was known as Algorithm.

Cybersecurity is the protection of computers from theft or damage to their hardware, software or electronic data. In October 2018, the Dutch government said that they had foiled a plot by Russian military intelligence to launch a cyber-attack on the headquarters of the Organisation for the Prohibition of Chemical Weapons (OPCW) in the Hague.[25]

The term **cloud robotics** simply means storing and accessing data and programmes over the internet, instead of using the computer's hard drive.

Big Data means that extremely large data sets may be analysed by computers to reveal patterns, trends and associations, especially relating to human behaviour or interactions.

25 David Bond, George Parker and Mehreen Khan, 'Netherlands say it foiled Russian hack', *The Irish Times*, 5 October 2018.

Chapter 1
The Impact of AI on Jobs

Alan Turing, one of the first scholars to become involved in developing AI, had Irish connections. His mother, Ethel Stoney, a member of the landlord class in North Tipperary was born in Arran Hill House located near the town of Borrisokane. Turing studied mathematics at King's College in Cambridge and completed a PhD there in 1938. While at the university, he realised that computers are very efficient machines for adding, subtracting and making logical decisions.

During the Second World War Turing worked at the British government's Code and Cypher School at Bletchley. While working there he played a crucial role in breaking the German military code. This helped the Allies win various battles, including the Battle of the Atlantic which many believed shortened the war.

After the Second World War, Turing became deputy director of the computing laboratory at the University of Manchester, where he worked at building computers, and engaged in pioneering work on AI. Turing was very influential in the development of theoretical computer science.

'Pepper' in Parliament

In October 2018, 'Pepper', a humanoid robot, was brought to the British parliament at Westminster to demonstrate how robots are being engineered to look and act like humans. The chair of Westminster's Education Committee, Robert Halfon, asked Pepper to introduce *him*self, not *it*self. In reply, Pepper said, 'Good morning, Chair. Thank you for inviting me to give evidence here today. My name is Pepper, and I'm the resident robot at Middlesex University.'[1]

1 Science and Technology, Humanoid 'Pepper' Appears in British Parliament, 17 October 2018 (https://learningenglish.voanews.com/a/humanoid-robot-pepper-appears-in-britain-s-parliament/4617564.html).

We need to be careful with the language we use when describing robots and algorithms. It is inappropriate to give a human name to robots or algorithms as it humanises what are merely sophisticated machines. While recognising that these machines are powerful and can accomplish complex tasks, we must be clear that they do not have consciousness or share human emotions or values.

The Fourth Industrial Revolution

We are now beginning to realise how powerful AI machines can be. AI recognises patterns and finds relationships in data that are so complex that no individual human being or groups of humans can see those connections. In January 2017, Libratus, an AI program designed to play poker, was entered in a twenty-day-long-tournament against four of the best poker players in the world.[2] Libratus won. Previously, AI machines had beaten humans at chess, and at a Korean game called 'Go', which is often regarded as one of the most complex games in existence. The algorithms that powered Libratus were designed to have applications beyond winning at poker.

AI is being used in agriculture, finance, banking, insurance, healthcare, education, agriculture, policing, retail, construction, trade, military strategies and in the care of the young and the elderly. These new technologies are found in every country across the globe. The office of the Revenue Commissioners in Ireland has stated that they will team up with Accenture, one of the largest consulting and technology firms in the world, to bring high-tech expertise to the tax system. Accenture helps businesses to redefine their strategies and to work creatively with the new technologies. In September 2018, they tested a voice-driven digital assistant that will help callers with their queries.[3]

2 Olivia Solon, 'Cards are stacked against humanity after artificial intelligence wins poker contest', *The Guardian*, 1 February 2017.

3 Ciara O'Brien, 'Voice bot pilot service to answer your tax queries', *The Irish Times*, 6 September 2018 (https://www.irishtimes.com/business/technology/revenue-turns-to-a-digital-bot-to-answer-your-tax-queries-1.3619383).

It is important to situate AI – robots, drones and 3D printing – in the context of the industrial revolutions that have shaped our modern world for the last two and a half centuries. The first Industrial Revolution, driven by steam, began in Britain after the 1750s. While it destroyed jobs on farms and the rural-based clothing business, manufacturing industries created many new jobs in the factories that sprang up in cities like Birmingham and Manchester. It also gave rise to a rail network, which helped move goods and people around Britain. Growth in international shipping made it possible for British industrial goods to be sold around the world.

The second Industrial Revolution began in the 1860s, when oil, gas and electricity were harnessed to power industry and transport in Britain, the US and Europe. In the early twentieth century, Henry Ford developed assembly-line technology in his car manufacturing industry in Detroit. This technology greatly improved workers' productivity. Ford believed that his workers would not only manufacture cars, but that they would also buy cars themselves, further stimulating the market.

The third Industrial Revolution began in the 1960s with the arrival of computers. This, too, had a major impact on society, as workers moved from purely mechanical technology to digital technology in the 1960s and 1970s.

The fourth Industrial Revolution is being driven by technologies such as AI, robots, drones and 3D printing. I will argue that the disruption brought about by our current high-tech revolution will be like that caused by the first and second Industrial Revolutions in the eighteenth and nineteenth centuries. The reason is that it redefines the very nature of work.

Not everyone accepts this analysis. There are those who argue that the present technological revolution will follow the same pattern as the previous technology revolutions. For example, when old technologies, such as coopering and typesetting, became redundant, new jobs were created. This book will challenge that position, and argue that these new technologies will lead to huge levels of unemployment.

The Future of Jobs

One of the findings in the British Government's response to the House of Lords' Artificial Intelligence Select Committee's Report on AI is that the labour market is changing, and further significant disruption to the market is expected as AI is adopted throughout the economy. As we move into this unknown territory, the forecasts about the growing impact of AI on job losses, job enhancement and new jobs, are inevitably speculative. However, there is an urgent need to analyse and assess, on an ongoing basis, the evolution of AI, so that adequate policies can be pursed in response to this new and challenging situation.[4]

In his book, *Why the Future is Workless,* Tim Dunlop predicts that these technologies will replace people in the workforce, and lead to significant levels of unemployment and impoverishment for large groups of people.[5] Terry Gou is a Taiwanese tycoon and founder and chairman of Foxconn, one of the biggest high-tech companies in the world, with factories all over China, making smartphones for many tech companies. In 2011, Mr Gou promised to buy one million robots to replace many of the workers whom he employs. While it appears that his automation plans are being implemented more slowly than expected, he is still in the process of reducing the number of workers he requires. At the end of 2016, the employees at his companies numbered 837,000.[6] One of the reasons why he is investing in robots is that during the last decade wages in China have risen significantly. As a result, it is now more expensive to keep a large workforce in China than it was during the past two decades.[7]

4 'Impact of the labour market, Recommendation 39', Government response to the House of Lords Artificial Intelligence Select Committee's Report on AI in the UK, June 2018.
5 Tim Dunlop, *Why the Future is Workless*, Sydney: New South Publishing, 2016.
6 Ziyi Tang & Tripti Lahiri, 'Here's how the plan to replace the humans who make iPhones with bots is going', the Quartz Daily Brief email, 22 June 2018 (https://qz.com/1312079/iphone-maker-foxconn-is-churning-out-foxbots-to-replace-its-human-workers).
7 Alec Ross, *The Industries of the Future*, London: Simon & Schuster, 2016, 37.

Early in 2018, online retailer Shop Direct warned that 2,000 jobs were at risk of being lost, as the company moved into a new distribution centre.[8] Economists fear that those on lower incomes or engaged in manual work will be the first to be affected. However, automation will also claw away at the jobs of the middle class. This will put huge pressure on government finances as income tax revenue will drop dramatically.

Not everyone would agree with or accept my analysis. A report from The World Economic Forum (WEF) insists that globally, about 133 million jobs will be created by these new technologies, while 75 million jobs will be lost. These findings are the result of a survey of executives representing fifteen million workers in twenty countries.[9] Their view is not widely shared by the many commentators who foresee major adverse changes in employment, as more and more workplaces become automated over a short period of time.

The Office for National Statistics (ONS) estimates that about 1.5 million workers in Britain are at risk of losing their jobs to automation. They estimate that women and those in part-time work will be most affected. These statistics show that supermarket checkout assistants, most of whom are women, have already borne the brunt of the introduction of automation in the retail trade, with 25.3 per cent of jobs in the sector disappearing between 2011 and 2017.[10]

In Ireland, many commentators claim that these new technologies could affect more than 40 per cent of jobs. In 2020, Heather Humphreys, Minister for Social Protection and Rural and

8 Jon Yeomans, 'Shop Direct jobs under threat in distribution centre shift', *The Telegraph*, 11 April 2018 (https://www.telegraph.co.uk/business/2018/04/11/shop-direct-jobs-threat-distribution-centre-shift).

9 Richard Partington, 'Rise of machines could lead to 133m jobs globally in next decade' – WEF report, *The Guardian*, 17 September 2018. (https://www.theguardian.com/business/2018/sep/17/robots-in-workplace-could-create-double-the-jobs-they-destroy).

10 Patrick Collinson, 'Women and part-timers most at risk, while supermarket checkout jobs fall by 25%,' *The Guardian*, 26 March 2019 (ttps://www.theguardian.com/money/2019/mar/25/automation-threatens-15-million-workers-britain-says-ons).

Community Development, believes that Irish workers face a 50 per cent chance that their jobs will be automated in little more than a decade.[11] A government report, *Future Jobs Ireland 2019*, predicted that secretaries, cleaners, taxi drivers, machinery operators and shop workers could lose their jobs. Taoiseach Leo Varadkar predicted that two out of every five jobs in Ireland will disappear, or change substantially, over the next twenty years, because of increasing automation.[12] If this happens in an unplanned way, it will have a massive negative impact, not only on the poor, but on the middle class, and this will be very disruptive for society, especially if it is not planned for in a competent way. This, unfortunately, is not happening at the moment. No section of Irish society, whether politicians, academics or religious leaders, are preparing quickly enough for such an outcome.

An Oxford Study on the Future of Employment

These issues are not confined to Ireland. In September 2013, Carl Benedikt Frey and Michael Osborne, co-directors of the Oxford Martin Programme on Technology and Employment at Oxford University, wrote a paper entitled 'The Future of Employment: How Susceptible are Jobs to Computerisation?' They predicted that many well-paid middle-income jobs were now at risk. Their research considered how feasible it would be to automate existing jobs, given the current and continuous technological advances that we can expect during the next few years. They examined 702 occupations in the US, and investigated how susceptible each one of these was to the impact of automation within twenty years. They concluded that over the next two decades, 47 per cent of US workers are at risk.[13]

11 Cormac McQuinn, 'Robots will take half of jobs unless we act – minister,' *Irish Independent*, 11 December 2018.

12 Michael Brennan, 'Taoiseach warns robots are serious threat to jobs', *The Sunday Business Post*, 30–31 December 2018.

13 Carl Benedikt Frey and Michael A. Osborne, 'The Future of Employment: How Susceptible are Jobs to Computerisation?' 17 September 2013 (https://www.oxfordmartin.ox.ac.uk/downloads/academic/The_Future_of_Employment.pdf).

The chief economist at the Bank of England, Andy Haldane, warned that fifteen million jobs in Britain would be lost through automation and robots.[14] An article in *The Guardian* in August 2018 referred to a study by the Fabian Society which stated that six million British workers are worried about losing their jobs, and feel that they could be replaced by a machine within a decade or so.[15] Less than a tenth of the workers think that the UK Government is doing enough to address this situation. Even among trade unionists, 16 per cent said that the trade unions in the workplace were not doing enough to ensure that technology would improve conditions for workers, rather than replace them.

The Gig Economy

The transition towards less secure jobs is already happening with the arrival of the gig economy, where workers are paid for the work they do, rather than for their time. Traditionally, the gig economy was confined to people working in the music and arts spheres. At present, it is being promoted by transport companies such as Uber, which collects and drops passengers at their destination. Gig workers are paid low salaries, and have very little protection when they get sick. While they work for a company like Uber, they are registered as self-employed. Many other employers are now following the gig model. Among them are Deliveroo, a food delivering company, and Airbnb, a company that arranges accommodation across the world. In Britain, the number of self-employed people has grown by 45 per cent since the beginning of the century. However, they are earning less than they did twenty years ago.[16]

14 Larry Elliott, 'Robots threaten 15m UK jobs, says Bank of England's chief economist', *The Guardian*, 12 November 2015 (https://www.theguardian.com/business/2015/nov/12/robots-threaten-low-paid-jobs-says-bank-of-england-chief-economist).

15 Richard Partington, 'More than 6m workers fear being replaced by machines – report', *The Guardian*, 6 August 2018 (https://www.theguardian.com/business/2018/aug/06/more-than-6m-workers-fear-being-replaced-by-machines-report).

16 Sarah O'Connor, '"Gig economy" panel eyes boost for workers' rights', *Financial Times*, 14 February 2017.

In Ireland, start-up companies such as Buymie, which offers on-demand grocery delivery, did well during the Covid-19 restrictions in the first half of 2020. The reason for Buymie's success is that it does not have the level of costs associated with large companies, which have to finance warehouses and delivery vans. Buymie is a leaner operation than other grocery delivery companies as it employs freelance shoppers who use their own cars to buy and deliver groceries to its customers. Eamonn Quinn, one of the investors in the business, expects that the Covid-19 crisis could signal a permanent change in the way that people buy their groceries. The company now plans to enter the British market, before moving into Europe.[17]

How AI Affects Workers' Rights

Some feel that with today's new technologies, workers' rights could be undermined, and that the gains achieved by trade unions over many decades during the twentieth century could easily be lost. In December 2018, the UK government announced that it would introduce the largest package of workplace reforms in twenty years. Much of it is focused at protecting gig workers from being exploited.[18] Workers will know what their rights are from the first day they begin a new job. They must be told about their eligibility for sick leave, their pay levels and their rights to maternity and paternity leave. While the unions welcomed some of the measures, the general secretary of the British Trades Union Congress (BTUC), Frances O'Grady, criticised the reforms because they did not ban zero hours contracts. She went on to say that these reforms will not shift the balance of power in the gig economy. This will only happen when unions get the right to organise and engage in bargaining for workers' rights in companies like Uber and Amazon where unions

17 Roisin Burke, 'Grocery service Buymie sets sights on Britain and Europe', *Sunday Business Post*, 3 May 2020.

18 Rajeev Syal and Heather Stewart, 'Workers get new rights for the gig economy', *The Guardian*, 17 December 2018.

are forbidden. At present, too many workers continue to be treated like disposable labour.

Beneficial New Technologies

Some of the outcomes of these new technologies will be beneficial as they have the potential to diagnose and cure many illnesses. In 2018, *Guardian* journalist Patrick Kane outlined how advances in prosthetics have significantly improved his life. He concluded the article by pointing to what AI and 3D printing technology has done for many people with disabilities. 'Blind people are having their vision restored by cameras, paraplegic people are learning to walk again with powered exoskeletons, and I can control my bionic hand with an app on my phone.'[19] Those developments show the positive potential of these technologies, and the life-changing outcomes are to be welcomed.

Questions for the New Technologies

Some claim that, instead of improving conditions for workers, the new technologies will push many people back into the situation which prevailed during much of the nineteenth century. They also feel that the large tech corporations have huge influence on politicians across the globe, and that the politicians must challenge the giant companies on a number of issues, especially workers' rights and users' rights. Many of these corporations are monopolies that should be broken up. Scientists for Global Responsibility, a campaigning group comprising scientists and engineers, surveyed its 750 members about the effects that AI would have on their future. Almost all of their members felt that AI would entrench and deepen inequality in society, as more power and benefits would flow to large digital corporations rather than to the ordinary citizen. Eight out of ten scientists thought that AI would lead to a dystopian future, rather than the utopian one

19 Patrick Kane, 'Being bionic', *The Guardian*, 15 November 2018.

that is often promised by companies if we use their technologies.[20] These negative outcomes will happen, only if people and groups in society are passive and allow large multinational companies to sell their wares, make more profit and prevent national governments from regulating them.

The Shaping of AI Policies by Society

With AI fast becoming a global phenomenon, it will be crucial for human flourishing that global and national policies control the development of AI, so it benefits society at large. We do not want to see these large tech companies controlling AI, and using it to shape society in a way that will benefit their profitability. This is the situation at the time of writing in 2020. The creation of algorithms, drones and robots should be shaped by values such as transparency, fairness and accountability. With the constant increase in the technical power of AI, its ability to learn from different situations, and incorporate that learned data into its understanding, it will be difficult to monitor or control AI companies without huge investment, some of which must come from the state.

Are New Technologies Safe?

With the arrival of AI and new high-tech technologies, many people had hoped that autonomous machines would make fewer mistakes than human beings and, therefore, lives would be saved. However, the October 2018 crash of the Boeing 737 MAX, operated by Lion Air in Indonesia, and the subsequent crash of an Ethiopian Airlines plane after taking off from Addis Ababa, raise very serious questions. It seems that, in both crashes, the pilots were unable to take back control of the plane from the automatic system.

According to the investigations into both flights, the single sensor attached to the plane sent data to the 737 Max software system which pushed the nose of the aircraft downwards, when the

20 'Beware of an AI-fuelled world', *New Scientist*, 17 November 2018.

automatic control system sensed that the plane was about to stall. Unfortunately, the pilot was unable to cancel the data from the faulty sensor and regain control of the plane.[21]

Many believe that, while human beings no longer exercise complete control over the operations of autonomous machines, they are still meant to be sufficiently engaged with the way the machine is functioning so that they can step in if it begins to function unsafely. This applies to self-driven cars as well as planes. Soon, accidents involving self-driven cars will highlight the same moral dilemma about who is responsible if a car injures or kills someone.

Conclusion

Those who work for rich tech companies have a serious moral obligation to challenge the behaviour of their global companies. In December 2018, 1,400 Google workers signed a letter demanding that the company take seriously the ethical consequences of its work. What was at stake was Google's decision to secretly build a censored version of its search engine for China.[22]

Another example of this is the fact that 4,000 Google workers raised the alarm over Project Maven where Google was helping the US government to analyse drone footage using AI.[23] Google promised not to renew its contract with the US military after 2019, to produce weapons or surveillance equipment. However, as we will see in chapter 9, some of Google's workers resigned when they felt that the company was not honouring that agreement.

As we have seen earlier, in June 2020, after the murder of George Floyd by police officer Derek Chauvin, Mark Zuckerberg, the CEO of Facebook, refused to take down posts by President Trump,

21 Robert Wright, 'Fallible machines and fallible humans', *Financial Times,* 15 April 2019.

22 Kate Conger and Daisuke Wakabayashi, 'Google Employees Protest Secret Work on Censored Search Engine for China,' *The New York Times,* 16 August 2018 (https://www.nytimes.com/2018/08/16/technology/google-employees-protest-search-censored-china.html).

23 Scott Shane and Daisuke Wakabayashi, 'The Business of War: Google Employees Protest Work for the Pentagon, *The New York Times,* 4 April 2018 (*https://www.nytimes.com/2018/04/04/technology/google*-letter-ceo-pentagon-project.html).

that appeared to encourage police to shoot rioters. As a result, many Facebook employees staged a rebellion against their CEO. Andrew Crow, the head of design for Facebook's Portals video-phone, tweeted: 'Giving a platform to incite violence and spread disinformation is unacceptable, regardless who you are or if it's newsworthy. I disagree with Mark's position and will work to make change happen.'[24]

In response to Mark Zuckerberg's refusal to take down President Trump's posts, Timothy J. Aveni, a Facebook software engineer, decided to resign from Facebook and LinkedIn. He wrote: 'Mark always told us that he would draw the line at speech that calls for violence. He showed us on Friday (29 May 2020) that this is a lie.'[25] He went on to write, 'Facebook is complicit in propagation of weaponised hatred, is on the wrong side of history. Facebook is providing a platform that enables politicians to radicalise individuals and glorify violence, and we are watching the United States succumb to the same kind of social media-fuelled division that has gotten people killed in the Philippines, Myanmar and Sri Lanka.'[26]

In the context of this debate, *The Irish Times* journalist Karlin Lillington asks, 'how much longer do we allow such monolithic speech arbiters – which they unquestionably are – to operate without limitation or responsibility?'[27]

24 Alex Hern and Julia Carrie Wong, 'Facebook employees hold virtual walkout over Mark Zuckerberg's refusal to act against Trump', *The Guardian,* 1 June 2020 (https://www.theguardian.com/technology/2020/jun/01/facebook-workers-rebel-mark-zuckerberg-donald-trump).

25 Julia Carrie Wong, 'Mark Zuckerberg defends decision to allow Trump to threaten violence on Facebook, *The Guardian,* 3 June 2020 (https://www.theguardian.com/technology/2020/jun/02/mark-zuckerberg-facebook-trump-protests-violence).

26 Ibid.

27 Karlin Lillington, 'Facebook looks increasingly immoral and thoughtless', *The Irish Times,* 4 June 2020 (https://www.irishtimes.com/business/technology/facebook-looks-increasingly-immoral-and-thoughtless-1.4270018).

Chapter 2
Algorithms and AI

The AI revolution, which started in the 1980s and 1990s, has given us enormous power to process computational tasks more quickly and efficiently. Now, AI has gone further and given these machines what we recognise as cognitive ability. In other words, it gives them the ability to learn, analyse, reason and apply previous learning.

Until these machine-learning processes were invented, humans were the only creatures that possessed this kind of cognitive ability. In the past, educational theories often focused on only one or two aspects of intelligence. However, in 1984, Howard Gardner, Professor of Cognition and Education at Harvard University, published his ground-breaking book, *The Theory of Multiple Intelligence*. He argues that each individual has a number of distinct forms of intelligence in varying degrees. These include the ability to sing, dance and play music. However, the ability to sympathise and empathise with others is also a distinct form of intelligence that must be valued. This presentation of various intelligences gives a much more complete and rounded understanding of the reality of intelligence than we had heretofore, where we focused almost exclusively on the ability to reason.

There is obviously an important connection between algorithms and some forms of intelligence, especially the ability to reason and learn from experience. Let us start with a simple example. In an article in the *New Scientist*, Timothy Revell gave an example of how different computers might make soup. The conventional approach would be to write out the soup recipe and let the computer follow the instructions line by line.

However, a machine-learning algorithm would attempt to find out how soup was made by watching thousands of soup-making videos and consulting thousands of recipes. Then, based on what it had learnt from this large amount of information, it would make the soup. This ability of algorithms to learn is extraordinary and will, no doubt, change the way we work and live in the future.

Initially, algorithms were considered something of a one-trick pony as they could crunch vast amounts of numbers at will, but could not move easily from one task to another or multitask, as humans constantly do. For example, an image-recognition algorithm may not recognise a speech algorithm or move to another area of knowledge, which is something that humans do automatically. However, this is now changing, and will change further in the future. In 2018, Google's RankBrain supercomputer used AI systems to help process its search results. These systems included image and speech recognition, translation and sentence analysis.[1] While this supercomputer broke no records, it scored 86 per cent in its image recognition abilities. This is almost as good as the more specialised algorithms.

Sebastian Ruder, of the Insight Centre for Data Analytics in Dublin, is very impressed with Google's new technology as it opens up new possibilities for the use of AI as a neural network modelled on the human brain, which can use the knowledge that it gains to greatly enhance its problem-solving capacity. Chris Bishop, Director of the Microsoft Research Lab at Cambridge, makes a very important point when he says that we are now moving from a software that is handcrafted to software that learns constantly from new data.[2]

Who Benefits from AI?

Some of the first groups to benefit from AI technology are those who have the skills required for writing computer programmes. A basic requirement is that they have a PhD in Mathematics.[3] In the

1 Matt Reynolds, 'Google AI reveals its wide repertoire', *New Scientist*, 1 July 2017.
2 Marie Boran, 'Putting humans centre stage in the AI race', *The Irish Times*, 20 July 2017.
3 Ian Sample, 'Hi-tech brain drain threatens British university research', *The Guardian*, 2 November 2017.

US, a software developer's salary averages about $100,000 a year, according to the US Bureau of Labour Statistics.[4] According to the jobs website Indeed the number of AI jobs in the UK has risen by a staggering 485% since 2014.[5] In 2017, there were more than two jobs available for every qualified applicant.

The downside to this development is that in Britain, elite universities are being stripped of their experts in AI by private firms such as Google, Facebook, Amazon, Apple, Microsoft and Twitter. These companies are willing to pay salaries three or four times higher than universities can afford to pay. This, in turn, is leading to a disruption in both teaching and research programmes at many prestigious universities across the globe.

The Irish journalist, Chris Johns, is clear that AI jobs are the top jobs of our time. Jocosely, he makes the point that parents who have encouraged their children to be doctors, accountants or lawyers, have all been mistaken! Furthermore, he holds that our long-held beliefs about the enduring value of the usual professional qualifications are also wrong. Data scientists tell us that AI is going to put many of us out of work in the next decade or two. Professor Yuval Noah Harari, historian, philosopher and best-selling author of *Sapiens* and *Homo Deus*, has probably put it best when he predicts that workers will no longer be exploited, merely irrelevant.[6]

Malware attacks

Though malware attacks are very destructive, I feel that cybersecurity belongs in the positive column because it is one of the areas that will secure jobs in the biotech age. In May 2017, a cyber-attack called WannaCry spread to over a hundred countries. More than

4 US Bureau of Labour Statistics, US Department of Labour, 'Software Developers' in Occupational Outlook Handbook (https://www.bls.gov/ooh/computer-and-information-technology/software-developers.htm).

5 BBC News, 'Artificial intelligence sector "needs more brain power"', BBC, 5 October 2017 (https://www.bbc.com/news/technology-41489643).

6 Chris Johns, 'Tell your children to forget becoming doctors or lawyers', *The Irish Times*, 10 September 2018.

100,000 computers at 30,000 institutions and organisations, which included government agencies, hospitals and internet companies, were affected. It is estimated that WannaCry cost affected users more than $4 billion.[7]

This is the reason that from 2000 to 2020, the cybersecurity market grew from a low base of $3.5 billion to $175 billion. Cybersecurity is now employed in all business sectors, big and small, and the number of employees involved has grown exponentially in recent years.[8] Guillermo Suárez-Tangil, of King's College, London, and Sergio Pastrana of the Charles III University of Madrid, have analysed more than 4.4 million incidences of cryptojacking. This is the secret use of computing devices to source cryptocurrency. In their research, they found that cryptojacking has generated an estimated $57 million worldwide since 2017. Hackers have targeted home computers, and many people fear that they will target the computers that control larger infrastructures such as power-generating plants. According to Suarez-Tangil, cryptojacking keeps growing each year and shows no sign of slowing down. It is expected that this problem is going to increase dramatically in the next few years.[9] A cyber-attack can be launched from any part of the world, and this can make it difficult to trace. Organisations need to educate their staff about issues around cybersecurity so as not to leave themselves open to data loss or hacking.

In May 2019, WhatsApp, which is used by 1.5 billion users, discovered that attackers were able to install surveillance software on iPhones and Android phones by phoning people, using the app's phone call function. Unknown to the user, the attackers were then able to install the software, known as Pegasus, on the smartphone. Pegasus can activate the phone's microphone and camera and it

7 Henry Bodkin, Barney Henderson, Laura Donnelly, Robert Mendick, CHIEF REPORTER, *The Daily Telegraph*, 13 May 2017 (https://www.telegraph.co.uk/news/2017/05/12/nhs-hit-major-cyber-attack-hackers-demanding-ransom/).
8 Alec Ross, *The Industries of the Future*, London: Simon & Schuster, 2017, 125.
9 Guillermo Suarez-Tangil, 'Are hackers making money with your PC?' *New Scientist*, 19 January 2019.

can livestream events. WhatsApp engineers spent more than a week trying to close the latest loophole in their system.[10]

At least twenty countries had invested in this Pegasus technology for important tasks such as rescuing children, preventing terrorist attacks and infiltrating drug cartels. The programmers and engineers who created Pegasus believed that they were helping to make our world a safer place, but, unfortunately, this was not the case. Two lawsuits against Pegasus claimed its software had been attached illegally to the phones of journalists, dissidents and critics of authoritarian governments, ranging from Mexico to Saudi Arabia. As a result, in order to protect their privacy, many politicians in various countries have stepped back technologically by reverting from their state-of-the-art smartphones and replacing them with older Nokia-type models.[11]

In Germany, during January 2019, the personal data and documents of hundreds of politicians were pirated and posted online. The illegally sourced data included information such as mobile phone numbers, addresses, internal party communications and even personal bills. Martina Fietz, a spokesperson for the German government, said that politicians at all levels, from MEPs through to the members of the federal and state parliaments, were affected, and that Germany's cyberdefence agency was studying the matter carefully.[12] On 8 January 2019, Germany's Federal Criminal Police Office let it be known that a twenty-year-old man had been arrested in connection with the attack.[13]

On 29 December 2018, the *Los Angeles Times* and other US newspapers were hit with a serious malware attack. This was first noticed on the previous Saturday when it was clear that the attack originated from outside the US. It affected the newspapers' computer

10 Memul Srivastava, 'WhatsApp hack allowed security spyware to be loaded on phones', *Financial Times*, 15 May 2019.
11 Mehul Srivastava, Robert Smith and Quique Kierszenbaum, 'The business of spying on your smartphone', *Financial Times*, 15 May 2019.
12 'Hackers target German politicians', *New Scientist*, 12 January 2019.
13 Ibid.

systems and delayed the delivery of the newspapers across the country, including the West Coast editions of the *Wall Street Journal* and *The New York Times*, which are printed at the *Los Angeles Times'* printing plant. Throughout the day, the *Los Angeles Times* computer engineers had to work relentlessly to quarantine the computer virus and stop it from spreading through Tribune Media's publishing network and infecting the news production and printing process.

In *Cyber Wars Hacks That Shocked the Business World*, Charles Arthur, a freelance journalist, says that hacking is becoming more common and more complex.[14] For example, the consequence of hacking a cryptographically signed communication that links a utility to a smartphone could be disastrous. The hacker could then seize control and threaten to halt the production of electric power unless a large bribe was paid. A few years ago, news of these kinds of attacks appeared only in articles in specialised academic journals, because they were uncommon. Now, they are quite common. Companies faced with ransomware demands must choose between paying money to the hacker or risking serious damage being done to their good name and their business. Again, this is an area of criminality that is growing rapidly. It is estimated that 70 per cent of companies pay the ransom demands, and, as a result, the amounts requested by the hackers are increasing dramatically.[15]

Governments Involved in Hacking

Some governments are also hacking into businesses and national security agencies. Many people believe that China is top of the list. Next in line is the US, followed by Turkey and Russia. After these are Taiwan and Brazil, followed by Romania and India. The final two countries listed are Italy and Hungary.[16] Hacking is now a huge

14 Charles Arthur, '*Cyber Wars – Hacks That Shocked the Business World*', London: Kogan Page, 2018, 248.

15 Hannah Kuchler, 'Wind farms and robots vulnerable to hacking attacks', *Financial Times*, 31 July 2017.

16 'Which is the most popular country for hackers?' Quora (https://www.quora.com/Which-is-the-most-popular-country-for-hackers).

business across the globe because it is much easier to hack and attack a country's smart infrastructure than to attack the country militarily.

A study conducted by London-based think-tank Chatham House found that the US, Britain, France and other countries with nuclear weapons are increasingly vulnerable to cyber attacks. The authors of the study, Beyza Unal and Patricia Lewis, cited the lack of staff among the military who were skilled and competent in high-tech areas. They point out that nuclear weapons were developed in an era before the development of computer technology and little consideration was then given to the potential of cyber vulnerability.[17] Eric Schmidt, the former chief executive of Google, believes that the US military has been 'stuck in software in the 1980s'.[18]

Cambridge Analytica

Companies like Facebook have been accused of misusing their powers and not respecting the privacy of their users. In 2016, at the time of the US presidential election, Cambridge Analytica, a British political consulting firm that combines data mining, data brokerage and data analysis, harvested the personal data of millions of people's Facebook accounts, without their consent, and used that private data for political purposes. The company emailed millions of conservative voters in the US encouraging them to vote for a particular candidate in the 2016 election. Initially, Facebook did not admit its role in the Cambridge Analytica scandal, until Christopher Wylie, a whistle-blower who had previously worked for Cambridge Analytica, broke the story in *The Observer* in March 2018. Facebook came under increased pressure to respond to what happened, and,

17 Dr Patricia Lewis and Dr Beyza,Unal, 'Cybersecurity of Nuclear Weapons Systems: Threats, Vulnerabilities and Consequences', research paper, Chatham House, 11 January 2018. (https://www.chathamhouse.org/about/structure/international-security-department/staff).

18 Kate Conger and Cade Metz, 'I Could Solve Most of Your Problems: Eric Schmidt's Pentagon Offensive', *The New York Times*, 2 May 2020 (https://www.nytimes.com/2020/05/02/technology/eric-schmidt-pentagon-google.html?action=click&module=Top%20Stories&pgtype=Homepage).

finally, it accepted that it was responsible. As a result, many people claim that Facebook does not respect people's right to privacy online. This has led to a growing clamour that legislators, both locally and globally, have an obligation and responsibility to put in place laws that regulate the online behaviour of very powerful companies like Facebook. The penalties for breaking these laws should be severe.[19]

Biases against the Poor, People of Colour and Women

In May 2017, a judge in Wisconsin in the US used a machine-learning algorithm to send a Black person, Eric Loomis, to prison for six years. The algorithm used was called *Compas* (Correctional Offender Management Profiling for Alternative Sanctions). It assessed the risk of reoffending, based on data inputs about the accused. The judge told Loomis, 'You're identified through the *Compas* assessment as an individual who is considered a high risk to the community.'[20] The algorithm contained the racist ideology that a Black person was twice as likely to reoffend as a white person.

Because most programmers are young males, women are concerned that AI might become the ultimate expression of masculinity and promote misogyny in society. The lack of women in important positions in AI was demonstrated by a survey undertaken by the World Economic Forum and LinkedIn in 2018. It showed that women held only 22 per cent of jobs in the AI workforce. The data also pointed out that women with AI skills are employed in data analytics, research, information management and teaching, whereas men are employed in more lucrative and more powerful roles, such as software engineers or as chief executives.[21]

The World Economic Forum report also warned that 'in an area when human skills are increasingly important and complementary

19 Kate Magee, 'Cambridge Analytica whistleblower Christopher Wylie: It's time to save creativity', *Feature*, 5 November 2019 (https://www.campaignlive.co.uk/article/cambridge-analytica-whistleblower-christopher-wylie-its-time-save-creativity/1497702).

20 Michael Brooks, 'Artificial ignorance', *New Scientist*, 17 October 2018.

21 Charlie Taylon, 'Concerns over huge gender gap in the Workforce', *The Irish Times*, 24 December 2018.

to technology, the world cannot afford to deprive itself of women's talents in sectors in which talent is already scarce'.[22] Ivana Bartoletti, a privacy and data-protection professional who chairs the Fabian Women's Network, addresses this same issue in an article in *The Guardian*. She is adamant that young women must query the outcomes of decisions made by algorithms and that, furthermore, they must demand transparency in all the processes that lead to the creation of algorithms; otherwise she believes women will be sidelined.[23]

Bartoletti also points out that women lose out on another front because the jobs that are about to be automated through the use of AI technology affect women more than men. For example, in Britain, 73 per cent of cashiers in shops are women, and 97 per cent of these are expected to lose their jobs to automation.[24] Bartoletti believes that it is time for women, not only to investigate what AI means for them, but also to make sure that, 'in the public discourse, women frame and lead the debate about the governance of AI, so that it becomes a force for the common good and not the ultimate expression of masculine control'.[25]

As an indication that the education system in Ireland may be beginning to take these important issues on board, secondary schools are encouraging girls to study STEM (science, technology, engineering and mathematics) subjects for their Leaving Certificate Examination, so that they can study computer science in universities and qualify as programmers.

Virtual Assistants

Virtual assistants can do a lot of practical chores. Alexa, a virtual assistant developed by Amazon, can switch on lights and the

22 Ibid.
23 Ivana Bartoletti, 'Women must act now, or male-designed robots will take over our lives,' *The Guardian*, 13 March 2018 (https:www.theguardian,com/commentisfree/2018/mar/13women-robots-ai-male-artificial-intelligence-automation).
24 Ibid.
25 Ibid.

television set. It can also start the washing machine, open doors, play music, provide a weather forecast and even read the newspaper. In September 2018, Amazon unveiled a microwave that can be controlled using its Alexa voice assistant. Alexa can also book a taxi or order a pizza. The device cost £135 in 2019. Soon, Amazon hopes that Alexa will be connected to the internet 'of all things', so that it will be better able to understand and anticipate users' wants.

People ask why is Alexa always portrayed as a woman? A report for UNESCO found that digital assistants such as Alexa or Apple's Siri are both entrenching harmful gender biases and encouraging sexual harassment. As an example, Siri's response to the insult 'Hey, Siri, you're a b**ch,' is a timid 'I'd blush, if I could.' When Alexa is called a 'slut' her response is a submissive comment, 'Thanks for the feedback', instead of responding with anger and outrage to this unacceptable sexist language.[26]

According to the UN report, about 5 per cent of interactions with virtual assistants are sexually explicit. Companies, such as Amazon and Apple, should be challenged to end the practice of making digital assistants female by default as they embody all the negative aspects of sexist prejudice. The present practice is based on the finding in almost all cultures that women's moral experience is both undervalued and underappreciated. Powerful tech companies should not be promoting these prejudices across the world.

As AI machine learning goes from strength to strength, people will be speaking to virtual assistants more than to their partners. The UN report also made the point that only one third of parents in Britain now read bedtime stories to their children.[27] A quarter of parents ask Alexa to read them. This increases to over 50 per cent when YouTube and other platforms are included. We need to

26 *'I'd blush if I could', Closing Gender Divides in Digital Skills Through Education*, May 2019. (https://en.unesco.org/Id-blush-if-I-could).

27 Michael Staines, 'Only a third of parents in the UK are reading bedtime stories to their children', *Newstalk*, 28 May 2019 (https://www.newstalk.com/news/bedtime-stories-children-862501).

ask if children will lose out if we use robots to educate and nurture them, rather than interacting directly with them.

Paula Boddington, a philosopher based at the Department of Computer Science at Oxford, believes that more gender and cultural diversity is needed in both the high-tech world and the academic world at large. At present, both are so homogeneous that biases can often slip through because there is no one, from other ethnic groups or women, to challenge chauvinist and often bigoted thinking. In order to address this, we need diversity in terms of thinking styles, personality styles and political background.[28] Customers and users of digital technology and platforms must learn how to embrace their responsibilities by reporting the misbehaviour of technology companies to the proper authorities, locally and globally.

Facial Recognition

Automatic facial recognition (AFR) uses cameras to record faces in a crowd. These images are then processed to create a unique biometric map of each person's face, which is based on the measurement of the distance between a person's eyes, nose, mouth and jaw.[29]

Facial recognition can play a positive role in some situations. In India, for example, it has helped police identify and return to their families thousands of children who have been illegally trafficked. In Delhi, police have used automatic facial-recognition technology to search photos for a government database called TrackChild. The World Wide Web holds the database of police reports of missing children and of children who are being looked after in childcare institutions.[30]

28 Tucker Davey, 'Towards a Code of Ethics in Artificial Intelligence with Paula Boddington', *The Future of Life*, 3 July 2017 (https://futureoflife.org/2017/07/31/towards-a-code-of-ethics-in-artificial-intelligence/?cn-reloaded=1).

29 Ian Sample, 'Facial recognition will poison our democracy and must be banned now, says Liberty', *The Guardian*, 8 June 2019.

30 Edd Gent, 'Face recognition spots missing Indian children', *New Scientist*, 5 May 2018.

Automatic facial-recognition technology has been introduced at airports such as Shannon, Dublin, Heathrow and Amsterdam Schiphol. The main selling point is that it will enhance our travelling experience and ensure that we will not be delayed in queues at the passport desk or other areas in the airport.

However, facial-recognition technology comes at a price. This surveillance technology tracks us domestically and internationally and is a serious threat to our human and civil liberties. 'Big Brother' is around all the time. During the Covid-19 pandemic, many governments declared national emergencies and discussed using technologies such as facial recognition or an app as a way of tracking the disease. Paul Reid, the Chief Executive of the Health Service Executive (HSE) in Ireland, said on 2 May 2020, that the HSE would make a contact tracing app available for people by the end of May 2020, to help a person who had been diagnosed as having Covid-19 to identify his or her close contacts. The Irish app will follow the German model where all the relevant data is stored on the device and not the government's database. Here again, the issue of privacy is paramount, coupled with the trust that ordinary citizens have in their government to respect their privacy.[31]

In India, many are very sceptical of the request from Prime Minister Narenda Modi for people to use a smartphone app to help them identify their risk of catching and spreading the virus. Indian author Arundhati Roy said that 'the coronavirus is a gift to authoritarian states', including India. 'Pre-corona, if we were sleepwalking into the surveillance state, now we are panic-running into the super-surveillance state.'[32]

31 'Covid-19 contact tracing app due to be launched by end of May', *The Journal.ie*, 3 May 2020. (https://www.thejournal.ie/hse-contact-tracing-app-coronavirus-5090759-May2020/?utm_source=email).

32 'India's Covid-19 app fuels worries over authoritarianism and surveillance', *The Guardian*, 4 May 2020. (https://theguardian.com/world/2020/may/04/how-safe-is-it-really-privacy-fears-over-india-coronavirus-app).

The Persecution of Uyghurs in China

There are also many uses of automatic facial recognition that are very worrying. The Uyghurs are a Turkic Muslim people who live in western China in the Xinjiang Uyghur Autonomous Region. They comprise about half the region's population of 26 million. They, and other Muslim minorities, are being persecuted by the Chinese government. According to Human Rights Watch, the Uyghur people are facing an Orwellian-style surveillance by the police in China, where information gathered by facial-recognition technology is used as a way to persecute them. In August 2018, a UN committee heard that up to one million Uyghurs and other Muslim groups in China are being detained in internment camps where they are said to be undergoing 're-education' programmes.[33]

Colm Keena of *The Irish Times* interviewed people from China and Hong Kong who believe that there would be consequences for their families in China if it were known that they spoke to the Irish media in favour of the democracy rallies in Hong Kong. Three of them agreed to be interviewed, but arrived for the interview wearing face masks, reflective sunglasses and baseball hats pulled low on their foreheads in order to hide their identities.[34]

The misuse of automated facial-recognition technology is not limited to authoritarian countries such China, North Korea and Myanmar. It is also happening in democracies such as the US. In an article in *The Irish Times* in May 2019, Madhumita Murgia recalled the surprise shown by researcher Jillian York when she was told by a friend that photos of her had been found on a US government database. They were being used to train facial-recognition algorithms and, naturally, Ms York wondered if this had anything to do with the fact that she worked in Berlin for a non-profit group called Electronic Frontier Foundation. When she accessed the

33 Roland Hughes, 'China Uighurs: All you need to know on Muslim "crackdown"', *BBC News*, 8 November 2018 (https://www.bbc.com/ne and would ws/world-asia-china-45474279).
34 Colm Keena, 'China Has "A Lot of Spies in Ireland"', *The Irish Times*, 30 November 2019.

database, she found that there were many other photographs of her dating from 2008 right up to 2015. During further research she discovered photographs of 3,500 people on this database, which is known as Iarpa Janus Benchmark C (UB-C). Iarpa is a US body that funds innovative research on security issues in order to ensure that the US remains ahead of every other country on a whole host of security technologies. Jillian York also found out that Noblis was the company that had compiled 21,294 images for the US government. Among the images on that database was an *Al-Jazeera* journalist, a technology writer and at least three Middle-Eastern political activists. There was a photo of an Egyptian scientist who had participated in the protest in Tahrir Square in 2011. Once again, none of the people on the database knew their photos were being used in that way, and none would have given their consent had they been asked. The photos Jillian York found on the database were available online under the Creative Commons licences. Search companies often take photos from the internet and store them in a database and, although technically this is not illegal or a breach of copyright, the current system is ethically quite unsatisfactory because it does not properly protect the privacy of the people whose images are stored in the database.[35]

Karl Ricanek, professor of Computer Science at the University of Wilmington in North Carolina is an expert on many aspects of automated facial-recognition technology. He makes the point that the technology is not geared just to recognising people's faces. He cited a tech company in Boston, Affectiva, which is building 'emotional artificial intelligence'. The company hopes to be able to determine from a webcam image whether or not someone in the shop is going to buy an item. As we saw in the introduction, Shoshana Zuboff challenged this type of advertising in her book, *The Age of Surveillance Capitalism*, because it is a fundamental attack

35 Madhumita Murgia, 'Who's using your face? The ugly truth about facial recognition', *The Irish Times*, 9 May 2019 (https://www.irishtimes.com/business/innovation/who-s-using-your-face-the-ugly-truth-about-facial-recognition-1.3882501).

on our privacy at a point when we are making important decisions.[36]

In June 2020, the CEO of IBM, Arvind Krishna, announced that the technology company was opposed to the use of any technology for mass surveillance, racial profiling and violations of basic human rights. After the murder of George Floyd in Minneapolis in May 2020, he called for responsible national standards regarding how facial recognition systems could be used by police agencies.[37]

San Francisco is the first city in the US to have banned police and other agencies from using automatic facial recognition because it is an intrusion on a person's privacy. The ethical teaching of most religions emphasises the need to protect human privacy. Therefore, religious people should oppose any use of facial images on databases of governments or large corporations such as Facebook, Amazon or Google, if the consent of the person who has been photographed has not been given.

Digital Governance

In 2018, the UN Secretary General, António Guterres, assembled a panel of experts to deal with digital governance and cooperation.[38] Even the digital corporations themselves are beginning to speak about the need for digital rules and conventions. Brad Smith, the president of Microsoft, has called for a 'Digital Geneva Convention' in order to protect citizens from cyberattacks. The CEO of Apple, Tim Cook, maintains that the US needs its own version of the European Union's General Data Protection Regulations, in order to protect personal data.

The Irish Data Protection Commissioner (DPC)

In May 2019, the Irish government reappointed Helen Dixon as the Data Protection Commissioner. This is a particularly important

36 Ibid.
37 'IBM exits facial recognition business, calls for police reform', RTE, 9 June 2020 (https://www.rte.ie/news/2020/0609/1146265-ibm-facial-recognition/).
38 Anne-Marie Slaughter and Fadi Chehadé, 'International regulation is needed for the digital world', *The Irish Examiner*, 1 April 2019.

appointment, since the Irish commissioner regulates the European operation of global technology giants, such as Google, Twitter and Facebook. Given the size of these companies, it is surprising that since Helen Dixon was appointed in 2014, she has increased the staff and budgets by a mere factor of four, when a far greater increase was warranted.

On 25 May 2018, the General Data Protection Regulations (GDPR) became law in every country in the EU. The regulations gave enormous powers to the data protection authorities in each member country. They could, for example, impose fines for violation of the regulations of up to 4 per cent of a company's global revenue or two million euro, whichever is higher.

Nevertheless, despite these new powerful regulations, John Naughton, writing in *The Guardian*, reports that there have been few large fines 'compared to the scale of the covert data-brokering marketplace that underpins the revenues of social media and other companies'.[39] Naughton praises the regulations as being robust, but points out that they are not being implemented because the data protection authorities in most European countries are at present under-funded, and therefore do not have properly trained staff.

An accusation was made by US website *Politico* in April 2019, that Helen Dixon has not tackled these issues with the large tech companies that she regulates. Dixon rejects this claim.[40] At the International Association of Privacy Professionals (IAPP), in Washington, DC, in May 2019, Dixon told the audience that she wanted the sanctions she levied to have 'precedential value'.[41] However, legal expert Daragh O'Brien feels that Dixon was foolish to have previously accepted the Distinguished Public Service award

39 John Naughton, 'Data protection laws are great. Shame they are not being enforced', *The Guardian*, 2 May 2020 (https://www.theguardian.com/commentisfree/2020/may/02/data-protection-laws-are-great-shame-they-are-not-being-enforced).

40 Aaron Rogan, 'Dixon: I'm not a soft touch when it comes to regulating the tech giants', *The Sunday Business Post*, 19 May 2019.

41 Aaron Rogan, 'Dixon's US trip aimed to show Ireland no soft touch', *The Sunday Business Post*, 5 May 2019.

from the industry-funded lobby group, the Future Privacy Forum (FPF).[42] O'Brien felt that accepting the award from an industry lobby group may come back to haunt Ms Dixon in the future. She rejected the claims that she was not moving fast enough on powerful tech corporations, arguing that it is not possible to conclude complex investigations in a few short months.

More problematic is the fact that the office of the Data Commissioner was listed by the Department of Enterprise as the body responsible for implementing Irish government policy in this area. O'Brien points out that the Data Protection Commission was set up under an EU treaty to enforce and uphold fundamental rights under EU law. The *Politico* article stated that the office was not independent of the Irish state, which is known internationally to be constantly attempting to attract high tech companies to set up in Ireland. In the introduction to this book, I mention that the then Taoiseach, Leo Varadkar, believes that many tech platforms are 'free riders' when it comes to displaying content that other media outlets have researched and published. Despite this, he calls the tech giants 'great companies'. Naturally, this is what has given rise to *Politico*'s suspicions that the Irish government and elements of the Irish state are 'in bed' with the tech corporations.

The best illustration of this closeness between Ireland and large tech companies is the massive tax bill for €14.3 billion that Apple owes to the Irish government. The tax bill was imposed by the European Commission in 2016, when it established that, over a ten-year period, Ireland had given Apple state aid worth €13 billion. Though Ireland denied this and opposed the European Commission judgement, it was forced to collect the fine from Apple, which it lodged in an escrow account. In September 2019, Ireland joined Apple in appealing the judgement in the European Courts. In April 2019, Minister for Finance Paschal Donohue confirmed

42 Ibid.

that Ireland had already paid €7.3 million in legal fees supporting Apple's appeal.[43]

The real challenge facing the commissioner and her office was ironically identified by Dixon herself in a statement to the US Senate committee in May 2019. She asked, rhetorically, how an office with only 135 staff can be expected to protect the data of half a billion consumers and, at the same time, keep watch over some of the largest and most powerful corporations on earth.[44] In 2020, the Irish office is investigating 127 cases, but it has a mere twenty-one trained tech-enforcement staff. The DPC needs a much larger budget and competently trained people.[45]

A privacy-focused web browser, Brave, made this point in a report published in April 2020. It claimed that the General Data Protection Regulation (GDPR) cannot be implemented properly because of a lack of money and trained IT staff. This is why investigations take so long. The report found that only six national data protection authorities have more than ten specialist technology investigating staff. Budgets are also small, with just half of all regulators receiving less than five million euro from their governments.[46]

In February 2020, Helen Dixon told *Irish Independent* that her office had hired specialist lawyers to assess what level of fines should be imposed on tech giants. She indicated that the $5 billion fine against Facebook in the US would be relevant in this discussion because large fines act as a deterrent for these companies. Ms Dixon said that fines are inevitable, but she would not say when this might happen.[47]

43 Ronan Duffy, 'Ireland's appeal over 14.3 billion euro Apple tax bill to get under way in Europe today', *The Journal.ie*, 17 September 2019 (https://www.thejournal.ie/ireland-apple-tax-3-4812351-Sep2019/).

44 Ibid.

45 Naughton, op. cit.

46 Karlin Lillington, 'Data protection offices need proper resources now more than ever', *The Irish Times*, 30 April 2020 (https://www.irishtimes.com/business/technology/data-protection-offices-need-proper-resources-now-more-than-ever-1.4241106).

47 Adrian Weckler, 'Data Protection Commissioner signals blockbuster fines for multinationals', *Irish Independent*, 20 February 2020 (https://www.independent.ie/business/technology/data-protection-commissioner-signals-blockbuster-fines-for-multinationals-on-the-way-38972780.html).

The Brave report is critical and points out that the Irish Data Commission hires lawyers on 'a modest civil service grade, trivial in comparison to the private legal salaries'.[48] In 2018, solicitor Simon McGarr, who deals with data compliance issues, tweeted that the DPC was offering just €60,000–70,000 for a qualified lawyer who 'will be regulating the richest companies in world'.[49] Those salaries might seem quite generous at first glance, but they pale by comparison with the salaries multinational corporations pay their legal and technical staff.

Conclusion

It doesn't seem that Ireland, or many other EU countries, are taking data protection as seriously as they should in a world dominated by surveillance capitalism and very powerful and rich tech corporations. By not taking their obligations seriously they are undermining the privacy rights of their citizens.

48 Ibid.
49 Ibid.

Chapter 3
3D Printing is Transforming Construction, Manufacturing and Medical Equipment

3D printing involves computer-controlled sequential layering of material to create a three-dimensional shape. Various kinds of material can be used, including polymers, cement and foams. Chuck Charles Hull created the world's first 3D printer in 1983. The device looked crude and he called the printing process stereolithography (SL). Another term for this technology is large-scale additive manufacturing (LSAM).

The full potential of 3D printing, especially in building, manufacturing and medical equipment, is only now becoming apparent. At the moment, research and innovation are moving ahead at an unprecedented rate, and many people believe that 3D printing could revolutionise several areas of manufacturing. In fact, some experts predict that 3D printing could mark the beginning of a move away from the present mass-production phase of technology, signalling a return to making products individually and locally. This would represent an extraordinary about-turn for factory-based industrial processes that began with the first Industrial Revolution in the mid-eighteenth century.

Currently, most products we buy are made in countries such as China or Bangladesh, where the cost of labour is significantly lower than in Western countries. In recent decades, as labour costs increased in developed countries, Western companies moved their factories to developing countries. This move has often exploited cheap labour by not paying the workers adequately for their work. This is happening today in the clothing industry in Bangladesh.

However, 3D printing could change this situation and further lower the standard of living for the poorest people on earth. This, of course, would not be good news for global efforts to create a more just and equitable world. Rajiv Kumar is an economist and founder of the Pahle India Foundation, a non-profit research organisation that specialises in policy-oriented research and analysis.[1] He believes that automation 'could be a nightmare because of all the educated young people who would be unemployed as a result'. According to the World Bank, population levels are growing so quickly in South Asian countries that one to two million workers could be added to the labour force every month for the next two decades.[2] Despite the low wages that workers receive in the clothing factories of Bangladesh, 'sewbot' robot technology is being developed by Software Automation in the city of Atlanta in the US. Their aim is to automate the entire clothes-making technology, which will lead to unemployment for millions of people in Asia and elsewhere.

An important benefit of using 3D-printing technology is that it will produce far less waste. Chuck Alexander, of Stratasys Direct Manufacturing Services in the UK, says that one of the inherent benefits of additive manufacturing technologies is that it reduces material waste by using just the material that is necessary to manufacture each item.[3]

3D Printing and Industry

In May 2018, Australian group Titomic unveiled the largest and fastest 3D printer in the world. Jeff Lang, the CEO of Titomic, said that 'only a few years ago people thought it would not be

1 Kiran Stacey and Anna Nicolaou, 'Emerging nations in South Asia and beyond are pinning their development hopes on creating millions of low-paid manufacturing jobs over the next decade. Advances in automation threaten to derail the plan', *Financial Times*, 10 July 2017.
2 Ibid.
3 'To do: Get faster, cheaper, more flexible and less wasteful', SME, 15 May 2017 (https://advancedmanufacturing.org/get-faster-cheaper-flexible-less-wasteful).

possible to use this type of printing process to make large-scale metal parts for industry'.[4]

In the early stages of 3D printing, manufacturers made small objects. However, by 2018, a bus-sized 3D printer had been developed. In the aircraft manufacturing industry this made it possible to create complex aircraft wing-parts, up to nine metres long. Gartner, a leading information technology research company, predicts that three quarters of all new aircraft will fly with 3D-printed components.[5] They are also implying that when a new cost-effective technology arrives on the scene, the product will be taken up quickly by other companies in different areas of the economy, because of its adaptability and low cost. Titomic is now in negotiations with Italian marine company Fincantieri about the use of 3D printing in their industry. Titomic refers to Fincantieri as a major player in all the high-tech shipbuilding industry sectors, ranging from offshore vessels to naval ships.[6] According to Milan Brandt, Professor of Engineering at the Royal Melbourne Institute of Technology (RMIT) University in Australia, '3D printing would remove the labour cost element in manufacturing by automatic processes.'[7]

Many automobile companies, especially those involved in building electric cars, are showing a real interest in 3D printing. One major benefit of 3D-printed cars is that the weight of the vehicle is reduced significantly. As we will see later, electric car manufacturers realise that battery technology is extremely dense and, therefore, heavy. Reducing the vehicle's weight increases the distance a car can travel on a single electric charge. In 2019, there were only 10,000 electric cars in Ireland. The Irish government's climate change plan, launched in June 2019, predicts that there will

4 Jamie Smyth, 'Australians develop bus-sized 3D printer', *Financial Times*, 17 May 2018.
5 Ibid.
6 Sarah Saunders, 'Titomic Brings Kinetic Fusion 3D Printing to Marine Sector with New Fincantieri Agreement', 3D printing.com., 14 May 2018 (https://3dprint.com/213496/titomic-signs-mou-fincantieri/).
7 Ibid.

be one million electric cars on Irish roads by 2030. Whether this will happen is open to question.

Adidas and 3D Printing

In 2017, Adidas, the giant German sports goods firm, built a digitised factory to manufacture sports trainers in Ansbach in Austria. It is estimated that the plant will produce 500,000 pairs of trainers each year. While this figure is only a tiny portion of the 300 million pairs of trainers that Adidas makes worldwide, this development will amount to a significant revolution. The new digitised technology involves computerised knitting and robotic cutting. 3D printing will make it possible for Adidas to speed up its production lines. It will also mean that the company will be able to make all the parts for the new trainers. While the factory in Germany will employ 160 workers, this is a minuscule number by comparison with its current workforce of a thousand in a single Asian factory.[8]

Nike, a main competitor of Adidas, is also planning to automate much of its production processes. The US company faces similar cost increases in its factories in Asia. Like Adidas, it also wants to shorten the time it takes to get new products to the market. Nike has set up what it calls an Advanced Product Creation Centre at its headquarters in Beaverton, Oregon. One of the tasks of this centre is to explore other automated processes, including 3D printing. The race between the world's biggest sports shoemakers is on, and automation will play a big part in the outcome for both companies.

3D Printing and the Oil Industry

It is very interesting that in 2018, British Petroleum (BP) began to study the impact of 3D printing on the growth of the oil industry. Consumption of oil may fall as the freight business suffers from the

8 'Adidas's high-tech factory brings production back to Germany. Making trainers with robots and 3D printers', *The Economist*, 14 January 2017 (https://www.economist.com/business/2017/01/14/adidass-high-tech-factory-brings-production-back-to-germany).

new shift to local manufacturing on a grand scale. If this happens, the growth of 3D printing could seriously affect oil demand. Freight transportation accounts for more than one fifth of total oil consumption, much of it involving long-distance journeys across oceans. Some of these journeys would be reduced if 3D printing moved manufacturing away from mass production, often in Asia, back towards local manufacturing in Europe and the US. Nothing is set in stone, but there are plenty of indications that 3D printing is facilitating a gradual shift towards localised and in-house manufacturing.

The trend in industry now is to move away from the long-established practice of sourcing products and parts from factories that are located thousands of miles away. In recent times, companies have used 3D printing to develop specific parts for their manufacturing businesses. This not only saves time, it reduces costs considerably. It now seems as if this practice is being adopted by many companies in different industries across the globe. During the Covid-19 pandemic in 2020, some of those who were affected by the disease were confined to hospitals and needed ventilators. This led to a major shortage of ventilators and respirators worldwide. An Irish-based company used 3D-printing technology to develop portable emergency ventilators, which helped save lives.[9]

3D Printing and Bicycles

A typical bicycle sold in the US or Europe in 2020 was probably made in China and shipped across the oceans to a retail shop. A start-up company, Arevo, is now printing samples of its first-generation bicycles at its workshop in Silicon Valley. These bicycles are made from thermoplastic embedded with carbon fibre. The bicycles can be printed and assembled locally, rather than being imported from China. The robot used can print all the dimensions

9 Karlin Lillington, 'How you and your (limited) tech can help fight Covid-19', *The Irish Times*, 16 April 2020.

of the bicycle and make the frame strong enough to withstand any difficulties the cyclist might encounter while on the road. The cost of the bicycles will also be reduced because the robots will do all the work and eliminate labour costs. The carbon footprint of manufacturing the bicycle is also low, since fossil fuel is not being wasted exporting the bicycle halfway round the world. Today, carbon fibre bicycles are made in a high-energy processing unit that involves baking the frame in huge ovens for hours, or even days. Using 3D printing means that a bicycle can be built for individual customers, incorporating whatever preferences they choose. Some of the bicycles will be made for taller people, others for those who are shorter. Some customers might prefer a solid-frame bicycle, while others might like a softer, more pliant one. In 2019, the first 3D-printed bicycles were manufactured at Arevo's headquarters in Santa Clara, California. It is likely that this will revolutionise the manufacturing of bicycles globally.[10]

3D Printing and Construction

3D printing is already transforming the construction industry. Dutch construction company Van Wijnen is using 3D-printing techniques to build houses in Eindhoven, the Netherlands. This is the first time that houses in Europe have been built in this way. The company said that it is adopting this method of building houses because there is a shortage of skilled bricklayers.[11] Rudy van Gurp, the company manager, says that 3D printing of houses will make the operation less costly because less cement will be used. He also points out that all the houses will have their foundations built in the conventional way. The company is working in tandem with Eindhoven University, a pioneer in the use of concrete in 3D printing. Van Gurp believes that within five years, 3D printers that design and build houses will

10 Adele Peters, 'Now you can 3D an entire bike frame', Fast Company, 12 July 2018 (https://www.fastcompany.com/90199960/now-you-can-3D-print-an-entire-bike-frame).

11 Daniel Boffey, 'Shape of homes to come: Dutch to build world's first 3D printed housing estate', *The Guardian*, 6 June 2018.

become quite common. 3D printing construction will mean that people will be able to design their homes to suit their own needs, instead of having to buy a standard house, as happens at present.[12] The downside of all of this is that there will be far fewer people working in the building sector in the future.

Robotic building sites are not confined to the Netherlands. In China, a firm called Winsun claims to have printed 3D models of ten entire buildings in just twenty-four hours. In Russia, the Apis Cor company printed the shell of a small concrete house in a day, although the building still needed a roof, windows and insulation. Various aspects of the building process have also been speeded up enormously. In Perth, Australia, a company called Fastbrick has developed a system that can lay 1,000 bricks in one hour. The whole operation is directed from a computer and the process uses glue instead of cement to hold the bricks together.

3D Printing and Medicine

For over twenty years, the medical industry has utilised 3D printing for creating some equipment. In the past few years, the use of 3D printing in the medical world has developed significantly. Currently, we use 3D printing for anything from dental applications to customisable prosthetics, 3D-printed skin and airway splints for infants. At present, a hospital in Jordan is fitting refugees who have been injured in the conflict in Syria with 3D-printed prosthetic limbs. This technology allows an artificial limb to be designed and built within the space of twenty-four hours. The 3D-printed limb costs a fraction of a conventional prosthetic.[13] One major advantage of the 3D-printed prosthesis is that it is much lighter than the conventional one, and is custom-made to the requirements of the individual patient.

12 Ibid.

13 James Holloway, 'How 3D printed prosthetic limbs are helping one hospital treat Syrian war refugees', *New Atlas*, 6 March 2018 (https://newatlas.com/3d-printed-prostheses-syria/53685).

However, the focus of 3D researchers has moved beyond producing inanimate objects and now has the potential to print vital organs such as kidneys, hearts and livers. Results may take decades to achieve as researchers realise that a 3D-printed organ must perform many different functions in the body. It must be able to replicate all the functions of a natural kidney, and ensure that the body will not reject the organ.[14] At present, researchers in 3D technology at the Wyss Institute for Biologically Inspired Engineering at Harvard University and the Brigham and Women's Hospital in Boston are attempting to create mini-kidney building blocks that will have many of the key features of natural kidneys.[15] The research looks very promising.

Conclusion

What I have described in this chapter are some of the current benefits of 3D-printing technology. Gartner Inc., a world-leading research and advisory company, is following the astonishing growth of 3D printers, which they believe has been quite significant. In 2016, there were 455,772 3D-printing units in existence, a 100 per cent growth on the previous year. It is expected that the number of 3D printers will reach 6.7 million units in 2020. The industry is expected to grow at a compound annual growth rate of 26.4 per cent between 2020 and 2024, because it seems that this technology has the potential to transform almost every aspect of manufacturing.[16]

However, in terms of employment, there is a downside, as 3D printing will also erode jobs. Today, if a person needs a pair of shoes, he or she will purchase it in a shop, knowing that the shoes have been produced in China or Indonesia and have been shipped

14 Sean O'Neill, 'How to print a heart', *New Scientist*, 17 September 2018.

15 Benjamin Boettner, 'Method for growing kidney organoids under flow enhances their vascularization and maturation, increasing their potential for drug testing and regenerative medicine', The Wyss Institute, 19 February 2019 (https://wyss.harvard.edu/news/engineered-miniature-kidneys-come-of-age/).

16 'Gartner Says, Worldwide Shipments of 3D Printers to Grow 108 Percent in 2016', Market Screener, 13 October 2016 (https://www.gartner.com/newsroom/id/3476317).

from these locations. With 3D technology, shoes can be printed in any location in the world that has access to this technology. 3D printing could trigger a revolution and end the practice by rich countries of outsourcing jobs to poorer countries where wages are low, something that has been happening for more than a century. Korea, Taiwan and China chose this pathway to development in the twentieth century. If it is no longer available to poorer countries, the impact on their economies will be huge. Unfortunately, it does not appear that global leaders, politicians, economists or religious leaders are grappling seriously with the massive changes that 3D-printing technology will generate, and the impact that this will have on jobs and society in the next decade or two.

Chapter 4
Robots and Drones

A robot is a machine that can replicate certain human functions and movements automatically. It can be guided by an external control device, or the control may be embedded in the robot itself. Robots have been around for a long time, even before the beginning of the computer age. When Ben Russell, curator of the Science Museum in London, was researching robots, he did not expect that his research would take him back to the figure of a robotic monk who could walk around, strike his chest, raise and lower a wooden cross and carry rosary beads. Russell was delighted to exhibit the robotic monk at a robot exhibition in London in 2017.[1] The robotic monk was ordered by King Philip of Spain (1527–1598) for his son, who had been injured in a horse-riding accident, and it was feared that he might die. He survived, however, and King Philip employed some of the best clockmakers in Europe to build the robotic monk for his entertainment.[2]

Robots Are Now Being Used in Countless Ways

Robots can perform many useful operations. A pair of robots has recently been designed to assemble IKEA chairs in just nine minutes. The set-up involves two robotic arms with grippers and force sensors that work under the watchful eye of a 3D camera.[3] The robots are programmed with information about how the parts fit together, and they plan their movements automatically.

1 London Science Museum, 'Robots, a major new exhibition at the Science Museum, explores humanity's 500-year quest to reimagine ourselves as machines', 3 February 2017.

2 Joanna Moorhead, 'Monk at the cutting edge', *The Tablet*, 25 March 2017 (www.thetablet.co.uk).

3 Leah Crane, 'Watch robots assemble a flat-pack IKEA chair in just 9 minutes', *New Scientist*, 28 April 2018.

Robots Paint the Sydney Harbour Bridge

Since Sydney Harbour Bridge was built in 1923, cleaning and repainting it has been an ongoing task. Traditionally, when the cleaning and painting crew reached one end of the iconic bridge, they returned to the other side to begin the process of cleaning and painting the 485,000 square metres of steel bridge all over again. Previously, cleaning the bridge, using a sandblaster, was a dangerous, dirty and laborious job. Since 2014, two robots, Rosie and Sandy, are now constantly cleaning the corrosion on the bridge, and repainting it.[4]

Service Robots are Becoming Commonplace

Scientists at the Fraunhofer Institute in Germany have developed Care-O-Bot, which can sweep floors, empty bins and walk the aisles in a shop or warehouse at night to check the inventory and restock the shelves.[5] With these new technologies, we are moving towards an internet-connected world where self-driven cars, smartphone-operated appliances and delivery drones will become part of everyday life. In 2020, robots can do household chores, and a humanoid robot called TEO has now mastered the skill of ironing clothes. This robot uses high-resolution 3D-printing technology and built-in cameras to complete the job.[6]

A London council is using tiny robots shaped like mini-JCBs, called Q-bots, to insulate old houses and prevent heat loss. Instead of having to rip up floors, the robots crawl under floorboards and spray foam-based insulation on the underside of the boards. In old houses, this insulation can cut heat loss by about 78 per cent. Similar technology could be used on old buildings in any part of the world.[7]

4 Chris Bryant, 'Automation brings dawn of service with a cyborg', *Financial Times*, 6 June 2014.
5 Ibid.
6 'Robot butler irons your clothes so you don't have to do it', *New Scientist*, 1 July 2017.
7 Tanya Powley, 'UK looks to tap fast growing robotics sector', *Financial Times*, 19 May 2015.

The Use of Robots and Algorithms in Banks and Shops

Algorithms and robots are being used for customer service in banks and shops. Many robots used in the area of customer service are designed to identify individual people through identity-recognition software. Some software can now respond to human emotions, as expressed in tone of voice and body language.

Japanese bank SoftBank replaced staff in its Tokyo branch with ten 'Pepper' robots. Pepper answers questions, offers suggestions and interacts with customers by responding to the customer's vocal tone and facial expressions.[8] Not only can Pepper carry out these tasks, it can constantly learn how to do things better and faster.

The Use of Robots in Education

In April 2017, *The Daily Mail* reported that a robot named 'Pepper' was employed to monitor student teachers in a school in Japan.[9] 'Pepper's role goes well beyond this. It is expected to help students who have difficulties with communication. Pepper's insights are accepted because it is learning along with human students, and, therefore, can evaluate their progress.

Rose Luckin, a professor at University College London Knowledge Laboratory Research Centre, has focused on how digital media can transform education. She acknowledges that teachers rely heavily on social interaction to support their students and, also, to ascertain what supports the students need at a given time. She is interested in using AI to show teachers and students the details of each student's progress intellectually, emotionally and socially.

Her research became very relevant in 2020 during the Covid-19 pandemic in 2020, when schools in many countries were closed,

8 Victoria Woollaston, 'The phone store run by ROBOTS', Mail Online, 24 March 2016 (https://www.dailymail.co.uk/sciencetech/article-3507541/The-phone-store-run-ROBOTS-Tokyo-firm-replaces-staff-10-versions-Pepper-emotional-humanoid.html).

9 Richard Gray, 'Pepper grows up! "Emotional" humanoid becomes the first robot to enrol at a school in Japan', *The Daily Mail*, 14 April 2016 (http://www.dailymail.co.uk/sciencetech/article-3540307/Pepper-grows-Emotional-humanoid-robot-enroll-SCHOOL-Japan.html).

and students and teachers had to rely on online learning. It was predicted that students who had good facilities for study and access to a computer would do well, but those who had to share their computer with other family members and did not have an adequate place to study would fare poorly.

Professor Luckin believes that it is not a question of a choice between teachers or robots as educators. She sees enormous possibilities for creative collaboration between teachers and educational robots. An AI assistant could manage routine jobs, like checking on attendance and, possibly, assisting with lesson planning for students. However, online resources need to be evaluated and tailored to the students' needs by competent teachers.

Classrooms could be equipped with language processors, speech and gesture recognition technology, eye-tracking and other physiological sensors which would collect and analyse information on each student's performance. Teachers could use this information to adapt their teaching strategies to fit the needs of individual students. In that way, teachers would know whether the students understood what was taught. However, many students might feel that such a level of intrusion by robots in their lives is unacceptable and would have a negative effect on their privacy.

Will Teachers Play a Coaching Role for Technology?

Some commentators envisage a more central role for educational technology where teachers would play a coaching role to the technology and not the other way around. Reviewer Clive Cookson has interesting comments on the views on education expressed by Alex Salkever in the *The Driver in the Driverless Car*. This book is highly critical of the current education system. He claims that 'there are few institutions that are as inefficient and broken as the traditional education systems of the world because we treat education as an industrial good, a unit of knowledge served up to the masses on a one-size fits all'.[10] He predicts that in the future a teacher will provide lessons at home through online processes. Cookson feels that while this system might help some, the vast majority of children need the social interaction and camaraderie that are found in the traditional school system.

Breda O'Brien, a second-level teacher in Dublin, reflects on the challenges facing teachers because of the remote learning situation experienced during the Covid-19 pandemic. In an article in *The Irish Times*, she wrote 'that going from that contained chaos (of the live classroom) to spending long days staring into the computer screen in my back bedroom is not easy. It is odd to take more than an hour to prepare a 10-minute video and then not having immediate teenage feedback as to whether it worked.'[11] O'Brien believes that from a student's perspective, those who struggle in the classroom will also have difficulty with remote learning. Study habits are hard to acquire, both at school and in a remote learning situation, because students are constantly distracted by the frequent intrusion of notifications on social media.

Some of the same frustrations with home learning were captured by the editorial in the *Financial Times* on 28 March 2020 during the Covid-19 lockdown. The idea of home learning is sometimes presented as eager students, supported by their parents, attempting together to unravel the mysteries of science, mathematics or history. This, of course, is far from the truth. In fact, it is more often like the video of the stressed mother that went viral during the Covid-19 lockdown who ranted on WhatsApp that 'if we don't die from corona, we'll die of distance learning!'[12] The last sentence in the *Financial Times* editorial indicates that, despite all these new technologies, teachers still have pride of place as educators. 'One

10 Clive Cookson's comments on Vivek Wadhwa and Alex Salkever, *The Driver in the Driverless Car*, *Financial Times*, 3 May 2017.

11 Breda O'Brien, 'Remote teaching plans don't just click into place', *The Irish Times*, 28 March 2020.

12 Editorial, 'Home schooling is hard even for the best of us', *Financial Times*, 28 March 2020.

lasting lesson many home workers-cum-home- scholars will draw from today's crisis is that teachers will never again have to prove that they are worth it.'[13]

Use of Remote Learning for Disadvantaged Students

In 2015, the United Nations Educational, Scientific and Cultural Organisation (UNESCO) adopted the 2030 Agenda for Sustainable Development. This is a plan for the elimination of poverty through sustainable development. One of the goals listed on the agenda is to ensure that everyone in the world has equal access to a good quality education. Specific targets include free primary and secondary education, access to updated education facilities, and instruction from qualified teachers. Some nations will have more difficulties than others in meeting these goals. According to a UNESCO 2011 report, approximately 9 per cent of primary school children aged five to eleven, and 16 per cent of children aged twelve to fourteen, were not attending school. More than 70 per cent of non-attendees live in Southern Asia and sub-Saharan Africa. In the latter region, most of the schools are not equipped with electricity, clean water or sanitation, and between 26 and 56 per cent of teachers are not adequately trained to teach particular grade levels.[14]

To meet UNESCO's 2030 target of equal access to quality education, the world needs many more qualified teachers. The organisation reports that we must add 20.1 million primary and secondary school teachers to the workforce worldwide. It is easy to see why using robotic assistants to fill some of these gaps would be appealing. It will a take a lot of time and money to provide robots to support teaching staff, while acknowledging that trained teachers are the cornerstone of any education system.

It is true that some of those supportive of the extensive use of robot assistant teachers point to the fact that the robots do not need

13 Ibid.

14 UNESCO Institute for Statistics,'263 Million Children and Youth are out of School', 7 July 2016 (http://uis.unesco.org/en/news/263-million-children-and-youth-are-out-school).

days off and will never be late for work. Administrators could upload any changes to curricula across an entire fleet of AI instructors, and the system would not make mistakes. If programmed correctly, the instructors would not show any biases based on gender, race, socio-economic status, personality preference or other considerations. However, those whose philosophy of education is underpinned by the Latin term, *educare* (to lead out), would have serious difficulties with such a narrow view of the essence of education. Discipline is also a central issue in schools today. One wonders how robots could succeed in ensuring that a healthy code of discipline underpins the school curriculum.

The Need for Holistic Education

I do not see the future of education as being robot-based. Education in the context of the Gospel of Jesus favours holistic education and not merely skills-based training programmes. All schools must attempt to create a learning environment where children are accepted as they are, and are encouraged to attain their full and unique potential as human beings, made in the image and likeness of God. Holistic education engages all aspects of the student's life. It is not focused merely on learning about ideas, but also encourages education in the arts, culture, science, languages, sport, ecology and religion. Schools that opt for holistic learning strive to encourage pupils to be unselfish and to use their gifts, not just to benefit themselves, but for the common good of other humans and the planet. This will involve working towards building a just, caring and sustainable society where everyone is welcomed, and there is respect and tolerance for other people's religious traditions and cultural values. Hopefully, churches will continue to support such schools. Educators are right to be wary of any attempts by governments or corporations to promote robot-based schools under the guise of offering better value for money.

Drones

A major breakthrough in drone technology came when scientists and engineers developed the ability to create detailed 3D maps from aerial drone photos. Flying at sixty kilometres per hour, Lockheed Martin's Hydra Fusion Tools create maps with a resolution of thirty centimetres per pixel. The maps show trees and buildings clearly. David Hambling, a freelance journalist and author based in South London, who specialises in science and technology, says that there is a drone for every occasion, from monitoring farms, to checking on wildlife, delivering pizzas or even assassinating people, as we will see in Chapter 9.[15]

Drones and Construction Work

In some places, drones are being used in a very positive way. In Japan, they soar into the sky while scanning the ground to decide on the best location for constructing a building. Later, at the construction site, massive diggers work semi-autonomously, levelling the land and digging ditches.[16]

Over the past three years, Skycatch, a Californian company, has supplied its drones to more than 5,000 building sites in Japan. Skycatch is now adding AI to this technological mix. Before the company began to use drones, humans would survey and map the site. This process could take a group of surveyors at least a few days to complete. It now takes the drones fifteen minutes to scan the site and create an accurate, three-dimensional map of the terrain. Furthermore, these maps are sent directly to the bulldozers and diggers, which proceed semi-autonomously with the tasks of digging, levelling and piling up the earth. The machines also have cameras and GPS that are continuously in contact with the drones.

Skycatch is constantly automating the whole process. Their training programmes use machine-learning technology to train their

15 Conor Gearin, 'Drones find their way', *New Scientist*, 30 July 2016.
16 Niall Firth, 'Drones control construction gear', *New Scientist*, 17 March 2018.

various devices. For example, it has used hundreds of YouTube videos to train diggers and other machinery to recognise and interact properly with each other's technology on the site. Soon, it will hand over control of the construction sites to smart autonomous machines.[17] Angela Sy, a spokesperson for Skycatch, believes that 'we're looking at a vision of the automated job site'.[18]

It is also claimed that an automated building site will reduce accidents. Noah Ready-Campbell of Built Robotics, based in San Francisco, claims that in the US 'there are about 10,000 reportable injuries around heavy equipment every year on construction sites'.[19] Apart from reducing accidents, manufacturers of these systems claim that increasing numbers of autonomous building sites is also being caused by a global shortage of construction workers. They quote a survey from the Royal Institution of Chartered Surveyors in Britain which showed that in 2017, 60 per cent of building companies were experiencing a shortage of building workers. However, while there might be a shortage of workers in Britain this is hardly true at a global level. In 2020, there are 7.7 billion people on the planet. Demographers tell us that the world population will be ten billion by 2070. This tells us that there will be plenty of people around in 2050, but with increased automation there will be fewer jobs.

Drones and Mining

At its Pilbara site in Western Australia, mining giant Rio Tinto is rolling out the first heavy freight self-driven rail network. Rio is leading a high-tech revolution involving trucks and drills that can be controlled from operation centres in cities, often far from the site of the mine.[20] Automated vehicles controlled by GPS technology are more precise and use less fuel than vehicles driven by humans. At

17 Ibid.
18 Ibid.
19 Ibid.
20 Jamie Smyth, 'Rio rolls out robot train after Pilbara pile-up', *Financial Times*, 23 November 2018.

the Rio Perth-based operation, almost 1,500 km from Rio's mines, there is a bus-sized computer screen that tracks the movement of Rio's 200 self-driven trains.[21]

Research carried out by business advisory company BDO, published as *The Near Future of Mining*, expects that more blue-collar jobs than white-collar jobs will be lost. They also forecast that by 2020 half of mining jobs will be replaced by robots. Some of the miners will be retrained to run and control the robots.[22] BDO's research points out that mining companies are quick to embrace high-tech solutions because this will generate more profits for them.

An underwater drone will change the face of the mining industry, if research funded by the EU, the Alternative Mining Operating System, is successful. The focus of the research is to extract mineral resources from abandoned, flooded mines previously considered too dangerous or too costly to mine. It is already being tested at the flooded Whitehill Yeo China clay pit in Devon, England. If the project proves successful, these mining drones will go global almost immediately.

Many people would regard this method of mining as a blessing. We would be able to produce new raw materials without having to dig new mines. Drilling and blasting would become unnecessary, and this would benefit the environment. Socially, it will be a blessing because it will reduce noise pollution.[23]

However, if drone mining happens, mining will no longer provide jobs for many people, as is clear from the Australian data. Tara Mines, the biggest lead and zinc mine in Europe, is located near Navan, County Meath, Ireland. In 2017, six hundred people were working at Tara Mines. It is estimated that there are enough resources to operate the mine until 2026. When the mine is closed, it will be a huge blow economically to the town of Navan and the surrounding area.

21 Ibid.
22 Ibid.
23 David Hambling, 'Underwater drone will change mining', *New Scientist*, 28 October 2017.

Food Delivery by Drones

A drone company that plans to bring food deliveries to people in their homes hopes to be operating in Ireland in 2020. The technology means that anyone ordering food will now be able to tick 'drone delivery' when ordering food through apps or websites. The drones are expected to fly at eighty kilometres per hour, and will deliver the food in less than three minutes.[24] In September 2019, an Irish start-up company, Manna, was attempting to get a licence from the Irish Aviation Authority to fly drones. Manna is in discussions with Flipdish, which was founded in 2015 and facilitates online orders from a variety of restaurants. Flipdish's chief executive, Conor McCarthy, believes that 'access to fast efficient delivery technology will be a game changer for the industry'.[25] The widespread use of drones for food delivery will destroy the current car and bicycle delivery business, and will lead to unemployment in the food delivery sector.

Drones and Insurance

In the US, hundreds of drone pilots are now surveying property damaged by storms or other disasters to check the legitimacy of insurance claims.[26] When US Federal Aviation commercial regulations came into force in August 2016, insurance companies began to train their staff to pilot drones in order to evaluate damage to property. Often, especially in the case of fire damage, a drone is the safest and quickest way to find out the extent of the damage. One insurance company, Travelers, now carries out more than 17,000 drone flights annually. They use DJJ Phantom 4 drones which are equipped with high-resolution cameras. Other insurance companies are following Travelers' lead.

24 Mark Hilliard, 'Manna and Flipdish partner to deliver food by drone', *The Irish Times*, 19 June 2019.
25 Ibid.
26 Chris Baraniuk, 'Drones speed up insurance claims', *New Scientist*, 21 July 2018.

Conclusion

Robots and drones are relatively new technologies. Yet we see that they are already being used in construction, customer services, mining, education and in the insurance business. It is clear that the use of these technologies will increase during the next decade, and this will inevitably lead to fewer jobs.

Chapter 5
Robots and the Future of Farming

The number of people working on farms has decreased dramatically in recent decades, especially in Western countries, including Ireland. The 1951 census in Ireland showed that there were 84,657 agricultural labourers and 140,175 members of farming families, together with 199,805 farmers, working on the land. In contrast, the Central Statistics Office estimated that in 2016, there were 160,700 farmers in Ireland.[1]

The age profile of farmers is also rising. In 2015, a National Farm Survey by Teagasc (the Irish agriculture and food authority) revealed that in 2014, the average age of an Irish farmer was fifty-seven. Teagasc expects the age to decrease in the next few years as young people in agricultural colleges return to farming.[2] However, just 6.8 per cent of farmers are under the age of thirty-five, while 2.5 per cent are older than sixty-four.

Dairying remains the most profitable farming sector in Ireland at present with average yearly incomes of €68,877, up 13 per cent on 2013.[3] Even though the price of milk has decreased in recent years, it is believed that many dairy farmers may purchase dairy robots. When drones, robots and AI are introduced into agriculture, they will further reduce the number of people working on farms. As a result, farming will become a lonelier and more stressful occupation for farmers and their families.

1 Eamonn Pitts, 'Farming labour force has been in decline for decades – time to reverse the trend', *Irish Examiner*, 19 July 2018 (https://www.irishexaminer.com/breakingnews/farming/farming-labour-force-has-been-in-decline-for-decades-time-to-reverse-this-trend-856320.html).

2 Margaret Donnelly, 'Ireland's average farmer revealed', *Agriland*, 27 May 2015 (http://www.agriland.ie/farming-news/irelands-average-farmer-revealed/).

3 Ibid.

Changes in the Past Fifty Years

In the past fifty years, enormous changes have taken places in agriculture. Fifty years ago, farmers were engaged in mixed farming, and raised beef cattle, dairy cows, sheep and pigs, and also planted several different crops. The farmer's wife and children looked after the poultry and contributed to the running of the farm. Such farms were classified as High Nature Value Farmland because of the diversity of flowering plants, insects and birds. Most fields would have forty to fifty species of wildflowers.

The Agriculture Revolution of the 1970s

Beginning in the 1970s, many aspects of farming underwent a revolution. Swamps, marshes and wetlands were drained, and many hedgerows were removed in order to make larger fields suitable for tractors. These activities reduced biodiversity dramatically. The large variety of grasses in the fields was replaced by three or four species of perennial rye grass, which needs significant amounts of artificial fertilisers in order to grow. On the economic side, Irish farms achieved a remarkable increase in productivity during the last five decades. After Ireland joined the European Economic Community in 1973, new markets opened in Europe and elsewhere for Irish farming products, especially in the beef and dairy sector.

The Influence of Farming on Biodiversity

Unfortunately, this kind of agriculture has significant negative effects. High-intensity agriculture reduced the abundance of most native species of flowers, grasses, birds and bees. On a global scale, agriculture has contributed to the fact that one third of the 9,000 known bird species are now facing extinction. Much of this decline happened gradually, and people who lived in towns or cities hardly noticed that it was happening.

On 2 July 2019, Birdwatch Ireland told the Joint Oireachtas Committee on Culture and Heritage that during the last two decades,

Ireland has lost approximately half a million water birds. This is a reduction of 40 per cent.[4] Recent decades have seen a decline in the Greenland white-fronted goose, tufted duck, goldeneye and lapwing. Birdwatch Ireland warned that climate change has played a role in bringing this about, as farms have become less hospitable to wildlife. In 2019, only 150 pairs of curlews remained in Ireland, down from 150,000 pairs in the 1960s. Other birds facing extinction include the corncrake, yellowhammer, chough, lapwing and redshank. These birds depend on insects for food, and there has been a dramatic reduction in the number of insects in recent years.[5]

The Destruction of Pollinators

Intensive farming and climate change are threatening the future of bees and pollinators. In the Netherlands, for example, bees are responsible for pollinating 80 per cent of the edible crops grown in that country. Regrettably, of the 350 species of bees in the Netherlands, half are facing extinction within the next three decades.[6] The Netherlands is not the only country where there this is happening.

The National Biodiversity Data Centre in Waterford, Ireland, published a pamphlet entitled *Faith Communities: Actions to Help Pollinators* (2018). The authors point out that, of the ninety-eight species of wild bees, one third are threatened with extinction across Ireland because they lack food and their nesting habitats are being destroyed.[7] The booklet makes it clear that faith communities can do much to save our pollinators by protecting the wildflowers and hedges on which pollinators depend for their food. Even those of us who prefer well-trimmed lawns are urged to let the dandelions and daisies grow. Other communities might create a wild flower garden

4 Joe Leogue, '"Stark choices" if we are to save endangered birds', *Irish Examiner*, 3 July 2019.
5 Donal Hickey, 'Alarming decline in insects', *Irish Examiner*, 3 June 2019.
6 Daniel Boffey, 'Robo-bees could help take sting out of insect apocalypse', *The Guardian*, 10 October 2018.
7 'Faith Communities: Actions to help pollinators', National Biodiversity Data Centre, 2018 (www.pollinator.ie.).

in front of their places of worship. Faith communities should use herbicides as sparingly as possible or not at all, and believers should educate themselves in this regard so that they can understand the importance of the pollinator-friendly garden guidelines.[8]

Because there is still a major threat to pollinators globally, scientists at Delft University of Technology in the Netherlands are working at creating robo-pollinators. These scientists are attempting to reproduce the complex aerodynamics of the fruit fly. They hope to create swarms of tiny bee-like drones in order to pollinate plants and flowers if the real-life insects become extinct.[9] The robot-bees that they are creating can hover on the spot and fly in any direction. Their wings are made of a lightweight film of mylar, which is the material used in space blankets. The drones are fitted with spatial sensors so that they can fly from plant to plant and not crash into each other. Of course, despite what scientists can achieve, no robot can replace insects.

The Decline in Soil Fertility and Increased Water Pollution

Recent studies have shown that Irish farms have suffered a drop of 40 per cent in soil fertility in just a single decade. This has led to fears about the viability of farming in the long run. Similar studies conducted in the UK estimate that if these industrial methods of farming continue, there are only a hundred harvests left before the soil becomes too degraded to grow crops.[10] This is a frightening prospect. Dr David Wall, a soil scientist at Teagasc in Ireland, makes the point that without a balanced mix of essential nutrients in the soil, agriculture, which is a big part of the national economy, will decline.[11]

8 Ibid.
9 Daniel Boffey, op. cit.
10 Lynne Kelleher, 'Farming under threat as soil fertility falls 40 per cent in 10 years', *Irish Independent*, 26 November 2018.
11 Ibid.

Nutrient run-off from farms reduces the number of insects in rivers and lakes. In June 2017, Dr Matt Crowe, Director of the Office of Evidence and Assessment at the Environmental Protection Agency (EPA) in Ireland, told a National Water Event in Galway that, while Ireland's environment was 'generally good', there were 'underlying issues of concern'.[12] 'While the worst of the rivers have improved, we have lost the best of the best,' he said. 'National figures mask what's going on at a local level. Of some 4,000 rivers and lake water tested, 1,360 or 34 per cent are at risk, often from multiple pressures.'[13]

Mechanisation Is also Central to the Agricultural Revolution

In Britain in 1920, only 3.6 per cent of the farming population owned tractors. However, by 1960, that figure had increased to 89 per cent.[14] Productivity in agriculture also increased. By the 1960s, farmers were producing more and more food for a growing population. This was seen as a major triumph, and the virtues of this new and intensive kind of agriculture were celebrated. But the costs, through the impact on land, biodiversity and water, were enormous.

Farming and AI

In 2020, we are facing another revolution in farming. This, too, will have a major impact on the environment during the next few decades. There are possibilities that this new revolution may be able to reverse some of the adverse effects of the last agricultural revolution, particularly in the areas of increasing soil fertility and biodiversity.

One might assume that farming would be immune to the

12 Paul Melia, 'Water quality in one in three Irish rivers and lakes is at risk of deteriorating', *Irish Independent*, 21 June 2017 (https://www.independent.ie/irish-news/water-quality-in-one-in-three-irish-rivers-and-lakes-is-at-risk-of-deteriorating-35850649.html).

13 Ibid.

14 John Thornhill, 'The return of the Luddites', *Financial Times*, 13 July 2019.

revolution that robots, drones and AI are bringing to so many areas of modern life. This is untrue, according to Dr Peter Mooney, a senior researcher at the Department of Computer Science at Maynooth University, Ireland, who insists that farmers must become more competent in using computers and software on their farms.[15] This agricultural revolution will be built on using AI, 'big data', drones, robots and automated smart machinery. Small agriculture robots will make it possible to abandon large scale mono-crop agriculture, and opt for growing different crops together.[16] Robots can make small farms more productive and, therefore, more profitable for farmers.

Dr Mooney gave a talk in Mullingar, County Westmeath, in 2017. He claimed that by introducing aerial survey drones to map weeds, crop yield and soil variation, wheat yields could rise by between 2–5 per cent.[17] Dr Mooney is certain that the cost of fertilisers could be minimised significantly by using specialised agri-robots capable of microdot fertiliser application. This means that the fertiliser will be applied just beside the plant that needs it, rather than throughout the whole field, and, therefore, it will not pollute rivers, as has happened in recent decades. The increasing use of herbicides has contributed to herbicide resistance. The Weed Science Society of America recently concluded that herbicide-resistant weeds have been responsible for approximately $43 billion worth of financial losses for American farmers.

Tillage Farming and Robots

Professor Simon Blackmore, head of robotic agriculture at Harper Adams University in Britain, argues that we can now use sensors to ensure that we only deliver exactly the amount of pesticide needed in the right place and at the right time.[18] His company is testing an

15 Claire McCormack, 'The smart farming revolution', *Farming Independent*, 7 February 2017.
16 Anthony King, 'Futuristic farming and the rise of ag-bots', *The Irish Times*, 6 July 2017.
17 Ibid.
18 Ibid.

agriculture robot that can distinguish between weeds and the crops growing alongside them, and destroy the weeds with a small laser. An area of leeks that would take an organic farmer an hour and a half to weed can be weeded by the robot in ten minutes.[19]

Many tractors now use Global Positioning Systems (GPS) and have the technology to communicate with the plough or sprayer. In 2012, Simon Blackmore predicted that hi-tech farming systems are the way of the future. John Deere's new combine harvester can now summon a self-driven tractor and trailer in order to transport the grain. German company Fendt has devised a paired tractor system. One of the tractors is driven manually, the other is a self-driven tractor that moves along an adjacent row and mimics the movement of the first tractor. This cuts down dramatically on the time that the farmer has to spend accomplishing a particular job in the field.[20]

These are just the first steps in a new agricultural revolution. Very soon, the new machines will not look like tractors. Blackmore believes that fleets of light-weight autonomous robots have the potential to solve the problem of soil compaction, which is a major problem in industrialised farming.[21] In 2016, Harper Adams University and Precision Decisions began research aimed at growing grain by using robots, a self-driven tractor and a combine harvester to harvest grain, without a human being setting foot on that particular hectare of land. By 2019, the researchers had already harvested two crops.[22]

Dairy Farming

Smart farming is not confined to tillage farming. At the moment, thousands of dairy cows are being milked by robots.[23] Monitoring animal health and well-being through sensors and mobile phones can increase animal survival rates and the volume of milk they

19 Ibid.
20 Ibid.
21 Ibid.
22 Chris McCulllough, 'Automated tillage moves closer to becoming a reality', *Farming Independent*, 4 June 2019.
23 James Mitchell Crow, 'Down on the robofarm', *New Scientist*, 27 October 2017.

produce by at least 10 per cent.[24] In 2014, Lely, a Dutch family-owned business, installed 20,000 milking robots at a cost of little more than £100,000. A single robot can milk about sixty to seventy cows. Milking robots use laser technology to generate a 3D image of the cow. Each cow has an electronic tag, allowing the robot to identify the individual cow. The robot also knows exactly how much milk each individual cow is producing.

Most dairy farms in Ireland are family farms. Cows are generally milked twice a day, in the morning and evening. Using robots, cows can be milked three or four times per day. The deputy director of Lely, Serge Loosveld, points out that the cows are more at ease when there is less human intervention. It would appear that if a cow has a choice of being milked by a human or a robot, the robot wins every time.[25]

Sensors on animals, such as cows, can text the farmer when they are about to deliver their calves. Dr Mooney called attention to the app Moocall Calving Sensor, which currently records tail movement and patterns of spinal contraction as an indication that the cow is ready to calve.[26] Today, some of these apps are quite expensive, but Dr Mooney expects that within a few years, the costs will reduce considerably.

Farming and Water Usage

Researchers believe that robotic engineering systems could cut water usage by up to 50 per cent.[27] Robotic irrigation, like the microdot fertiliser system, will deliver water directly to the plants and not irrigate the complete field. The machine will also know how much water the plants need, and because it is connected to 'cloud computing', it will have real-time information on weather in the

24 Claire McCormack, op. cit.
25 Chris Bryant, 'Milking agrobots win the day with cows', *Financial Times*, 6 June 2014.
26 Ryan McBride, 'Why Mooncall calving sensor and Breedmanager app are great together' (https://moocall.com/blogs/calving/why-moocall-calving-sensor-and-breedmanager-app-are-great-together).
27 Stephen Gossett, 'Farming and Agriculture Robots', Built In, July 20th 2019 (https://builtin.com/robotics/farming-agricultural-robots).

area so, depending on the weather forecast, it will know whether or not to water the plants. Will farmers adopt these new robot technologies? Naturally, the economic cost of robotic machinery will be crucial. In 2020, the numbers of robots and drones that are available have increased considerably. Some of these robots will significantly reduce the cost of herbicides and insecticides for the farmer.

Automated Farm Work

Linda Calvin, an economist with the US Department of Agriculture, and Philip Martine from the University of California, have researched whether or not farmers will adopt these new technologies. They point to the response of raisin farmers to the bumper raisin harvest in California in 2000, which caused prices to crash and squeezed farmers' profit margins. The farmers realised that labour amounted to 42 per cent of their costs, and that particular realisation drove them to begin using mechanical harvesters. By 2007, almost half of the raisin crop in California was mechanically harvested. Consequently, the labour force has fallen in recent years.

In 2014, the US Department of Agriculture invested $45 million in the funding of research on automated farm work.[28] The purpose of the research was to create robots that can harvest berries and fruits. Over the next five years, a research team headed by Manoj Karkee from Washington State University will research the development of a robot that is able to pick apples. Apples are big business – the state of Washington alone produces seventeen billion apples each year. Today, each apple is picked by hand.[29] Karkee argues that the use of robots to pick other fruits will be commonplace in the near future.[30] Compared with other fruits, picking apples is not the

28 Ibid.

29 Qin Zhang, Manoj Karkee Amy Tabb, 'The use of agricultural robots in orchard management', in Robotics and automation for improving agriculture, June 2019 (https://www.researchgate.net/publication/334241592_The_use_of_ agricultural_robots_in_orchard_ management.)

30 'Robot apple pickers in the US could be just around the corner', *The Daily Beast*, 27 May 2019 (https://www.freshplaza.com/article/9106561/robot-apple-pickers-in-the-us-could-be-just-around-the-corner).

greatest challenge for those who are designing agricultural robots, considering the simple shape of the fruit and the fact that they don't bruise easily. According to Karkee, developing robotic hands that can properly handle more complex and more delicate fruit is still quite difficult.

In Belgium, a start-up company, Octinion, is developing a robot designed to pick strawberries and, possibly, other soft fruits. Pilot tests were carried out at their research centre in Hoogstraten in 2018, and the company began to sell the robot in 2019. The robot will use machine vision to locate ripe, flawless berries. Then a 3D-printed hand will gently pick the ripe fruit and place it in a basket. If the strawberry is not ripe, the robot estimates how much longer it will take before the fruit ripens and is ready for harvesting.[31]

Now that Britain has left the EU, the situation for fruit-pickers there will be similar to that obtaining in California in the US. This will make it more difficult to hire workers from Eastern Europe to harvest fruit, as happened in the past.[32] Because of these uncertainties, larger fruit-growing companies, such as Hall Hunter, which supply raspberries, strawberries, blackberries and blueberries to Tesco, Marks & Spencer and Waitrose, are working with robotic engineers to develop a berry-picking machine. The robot they are currently working with was developed by Dr Martin Stoelen, a lecturer in robotics at Plymouth University. He hopes that by tackling one of the most difficult soft fruits first, he will be able to tweak the technology so the robots can eventually be used to pick other fruits and even vegetables.[33] The robot that is currently being used costs £700,000. The final version is expected to be ready in late 2020. It will have four grippers, each of which will pick the fruit simultaneously. Though the initial cost of the technology is high,

31 Adele Peters, 'This Strawberry-Picking Robot Gently Picks The Ripest Berries With Its Robo-Hand', *Fast Company*, 29 September 2017 (https://www.fastcompany.com/40473583/this-strawberry-picking-robot-gently-picks-the-ripest-berries-with-its-robo-hand).

32 Ibid.

33 Julia Kollewe and Rob Davies, 'Robocrop: world's first raspberry-picking robot set to work', *The Guardian*, 26 May 2019.

the robot does not get tired, so it can pick fruit for twenty hours each day. Robot berry-pickers will have a major impact on seasonal employment in many parts of the world.

At the height of the Covid-19 pandemic in April 2020, Irish fruit company Keelings was criticised for flying strawberry-pickers from Bulgaria to pick fruit in Dublin and Wexford. Ryanair was also criticised for flying the fruit-pickers to Ireland. As robots are further developed to pick soft fruit and the price of the technology falls, this kind of controversy may not arise in the future.

Years ago, a secondary school or university student might spend a few weeks picking tomatoes to earn some money during the holidays. That possibility will not be there in the future because the Japanese company Panasonic has manufactured a new tomato-harvesting gadget that uses robots. The device runs along a rail and employs AI and image-recognition algorithms to identify the position, colour and shape of the tomatoes. It will harvest only those tomatoes that are almost ripe and ready for the market. It uses 'special effectors', which ensure that the tomatoes are not damaged in any way. In terms of the speed of the process, the robot is able to pick tomatoes at a rate of ten every minute, which is slightly slower than the rate a human can achieve. On the other hand, unlike the human worker, the robot works continuously, day and night. Panasonic had been working on its tomato-picking robot for some time.[34]

AI on Indian Farms

AI is also helping farmers in countries such as India. In 2017, Microsoft led a project in India that was aimed at helping farmers to increase the yield of their farms. The experiment used machine learning to predict when sowing and harvesting should take place, utilising historical data and weather reports taken over a prolonged

34 Luke Dormehl, 'Panasonic built a robot gentle enough to pick tomatoes, but not exactly graceful', *Digital Trends*, 2 January 2018 (https://www.digitaltrends.com/cool-tech/tomatoes-picker-robot/).

period of time. The company guaranteed the farmers who engaged with the process that they would not lose out if they followed the instructions from Microsoft. The farmers took the advice and planted their crop two weeks later than their neighbours who were not part of the experiment. At the end of the project, the yield of the farmers who participated in the experiment was 30 per cent higher yield than that of the farmers who were not part of the programme.[35]

Other Uses for Robots

In 2014, Hackney Nursery in Northern California ordered its first batch of robots. The nursery specialises in ornamental and perennial plants that grow in large tubs. In any one day, 5,000 of these plants might have to be moved around, and this heavy lifting and backbreaking work required four staff members. The management bought four robots solely to move the plants. To their surprise, they found that one robot did the work of four people.[36] The owner, Joseph Hackney, is delighted that the robots do this heavy and dangerous work which employees disliked.

There is another reason for investing in these robots. Most of this kind of heavy work was traditionally done by migrants from Mexico. In recent times, their numbers have been decreasing for a variety of reasons. Research conducted by Edward Taylor and his colleagues at the University of California, Davis and the College of Mexico in Mexico City, indicates that this shortage of workers will worsen in the years ahead. The immigration policies of former President Donald Trump has also slowed down the numbers of migrants coming from Mexico and other places.

Farm Robots in Japan

Many believe that the age profile of farmers around the world will drive the robot revolution on farms. Japan is a good example of

35 'From cows to cancer; the many benefits of AI', *The Irish Times*, 6 December 2018.
36 Aviva Rutkin, 'Green robo-fingers', *New Scientist*, 21 June 2014.

this trend. Because of low birth rates in recent decades, the biggest cohort of the population is aged fifty or more. This has led to a shrinking pool of agricultural workers and, as a result, Japan is turning to robots to increase food production at home.[37] In 2018, Japan produced just 40 per cent of the food it consumes. The government is keen to increase that to 50 per cent, especially by using more agricultural robots. In pursuit of this goal, Japan's Ministry of Agriculture, Forestry and Fisheries has invested $8 million over five years in developing agricultural robots. Noboru Noguchi, at Hokkaido University, is leading this five-year programme. The goal is to automate every aspect of farming, from planting through to harvesting. It will focus on the staple crops of Japan, which are rice, wheat and soya.

Robots are Taking Over in the Food Supply Business

Ocado, a British online supermarket based in Hadfield, delivers food for Waitrose and Morrisons. In contrast to its main competitors, it has no chain of stores on the high street so all home deliveries are carried out from its warehouses. Ocado has been voted the best online supermarket in the UK by *Which?* readers every year since 2010. In 2017, it tested a robot hand that could pick and pack fruit and vegetables. Ocado has found that the various shapes and textures of fruit and vegetables mean that these products are susceptible to damage and bruising when handled.[38] Like Octinion in Belgium, Ocado is now interested in acquiring two machines with robotic hands which have been developed by Technische Universität, in Berlin. These robots use machine learning and 3D sensors to help them gently grasp delicate items, such as eggs. If Ocado is successful in developing its robotic hand, and begins to use it extensively in its warehouses, what will the future hold for the 4,000 employees who currently work there?

37 Ibid.
38 Sarah Butler, 'Ocado tests robot with soft touch to handle fruit', *The Guardian*, 1 February 2017.

As the cost of agriculture robots decreases, farmers will begin to use them for several reasons. For decades, farming has not been regarded as an interesting and prestigious type of work, even though it supplies us with our food. Traditionally, it was physically demanding and involved long hours. This is one of the reasons why people from a farming background have migrated to the cities and taken jobs in factories and in the service industries.

Rising labour costs have also driven the use and expansion of robotic technology. It has been estimated that labour expenses on US farms amount to 42 per cent of total income. This is another reason why farmers are beginning to buy this new robotic technology. It is expected that sales for agriculture drones will exceed $1 billion by 2024.[39]

Conclusion

Farming has been shedding jobs since the beginning of the first Industrial Revolution in the eighteenth century. The introduction of robots and drones into farming and food distribution centres will continue in the next decade and will further reduce the opportunity of securing adequately paid work on farms. So, once again, it seems obvious that there will be a huge decrease in the numbers of human beings working on farms.

Fewer people working on farms in the future will further increase the level of loneliness and stress that farmers already feel today because of lack of companionship. Throughout the day, farmers will be interacting with robots, drones and machine learning, and may not have a conversation with another human being unless someone visits or calls them on the phone. Will this, in turn, lead to stress and mental health issues? With whom will farmers share the joy of witnessing the birth of a calf or lamb, if there is no social

39 Lauran Elsden, 'Drones and Farming', *Country Living*, May 2018.

interaction? These are major questions that society needs to address in the near future.

Farming families were central to church life for centuries. Will the churches be able to respond to the new reality that is facing farmers? How will pastoral practice be shaped and developed in many parishes to respond to this new challenge? The response will call for new fresh levels of social inventiveness, and the churches and religions must play their part.

Chapter 6
The Impact of AI on Caring for Children, the Elderly and Those with Special Needs

In the modern world, finding trained and dedicated people to care for the young, those with special needs and the elderly is a growing concern, especially in developed countries. Many of those who work in care homes or nursing homes in Europe or the US are migrants from Nigeria, the Philippines, Eastern Europe or Central and South America. Often, they do not have citizenship in the countries in which they work and are frequently held in low esteem. At least they were until the Covid-19 pandemic struck in 2020.

Japan has the oldest population of any developed country. A quarter of Japan's population is over sixty-five, and the number of people of working age is shrinking by 2 per cent each year. According to a 2015 report by Merrill Lynch, Japan will need 2.5 million care workers by 2025. This will be difficult to achieve because of laws that hinder the permanent migration of people from South East Asia to Japan. In 2018, there was a shortfall of 380,000 care workers in Japan. That is why both the Japanese government and the care industry are pouring vast amounts of money into manufacturing robots that can be used in childcare centres and nursing homes.[1]

Robots in Nursing homes and Crèches

A home-care robot called 'Chapit', which looks like a mouse, can sit at a person's bedside and engage in rudimentary conversation with an older person. Another robot, 'Robear', has the appearance of a bear, and can lift a patient from the bed to a wheelchair and, later,

1 Leo Lewis, 'Can robots make up for Japan's care home shortfall?' *Financial Times*, 18 October 2017 (https://www.ft.com/content/418ffd08-9e10-11e7-8b50-0b9f565a23e1).

return the patient to bed. The creators of these machines are hoping that they will be very useful in nursing homes across the developed world, because lifting people in and out of bed can cause injury to a carer's back and to the patient.

'Palro', a small humanoid robot, can lead a group of elderly people in exercise routines a number of times each day. In addition, the care robot can run quizzes which break the monotony experienced by many older people in nursing homes. All of these activities are helpful because they stimulate the residents, and this is good for their physical and mental health. At the Shin-tomi nursing home in Tokyo, a robot called 'Pepper' is used to care for and entertain the residents. Pepper can also monitor the corridors during the night, and this means that the homes do not have to employ security staff.[2]

AI in Animal Therapy

Many recent studies highlight the value of animal therapy for those living in nursing homes. However, in practical terms, this is often difficult to achieve because of the problems associated with caring for live animals in a nursing home environment. Toymaker Hasbro Inc. is a US multinational toy and game company. The company received a three-year million-dollar grant from the National Science Foundation to add AI to their robotic cat. The robotic cat is designed to act as a companion for elderly people. It purrs and meows, and even appears to lick its paws and roll over on its back, and indicate that it needs a belly rub.[3] The current cost of a robotic cat is $100. It has been found to reduce patient stress, stimulate interactions with other patients and caregivers and, overall, it has been shown to have a positive psychological effect on patients. It also works well with people who have Alzheimer's disease.

Complex robots are also being presented as a high-tech solution for staffing at daycare centres for children. Such centres utilise four

2 John Harris, 'Robo-carers might work, but they threaten our humanity', *The Guardian*, 2 July 2018.

3 Ibid.

robots, with one human supervising all four. It is estimated that they can assist in the management of up to sixty children. This is three times higher than the current child-to-staff ratio, and is one of the reasons why employers are so enthusiastic about the economic benefits of working with robots.[4]

Robots in Trinity College

In November 2017, researchers at Trinity College, Dublin, launched a 1.5-metre tall robot called 'Stevie', which costs €10,000. This robot cannot yet perform physical tasks for an older person, but it is able to engage in simple conversation and arrange video calls with family members.[5] The inventors believe that it can reduce boredom and stimulate mental activity in older people. At the launch of Stevie, Professor Conor McGinn of Trinity College, one of the scientists who designed the robot, said that it has many applications, including providing companionship for older people. The robot could also remind people when to take their medication, which is particularly important for those who have memory issues. Stevie can also be programmed to recognise what is normal and abnormal behaviour for an elderly person and, if something goes wrong, it will be able to notify a carer or relatives immediately.[6]

It is interesting that those who created Stevie worked with staff from Alone, an Irish charity that highlights problems faced by older people. Alone identifies loneliness as one of the greatest challenges facing the elderly in today's world.

In 2019, another robot, Stevie II, was developed by the same robotic and innovation lab at Trinity. It was unveiled at the Science Gallery as Ireland's first socially assistive robot. The robot was designed for care units, such as the Army Distaff Foundation, which

4 Roy Bishop, 'Robotics make baby steps toward solving Japan's child care shortage', *The Japan Times*, 1 April 2016 (http://www.japantimes.co.jp/news/2016/04/01/national/social-issues/robotics-makes-baby-steps-toward-solving-japans-child-care-shortage/#.V35w7bgrLIV).

5 Ciarán Darcy, 'Trinity's Stevie the robot offers older people help and a little light conversation', *The Irish Times*, 14 November 2017.

6 Kevin Courtney, 'How automations are infiltrating the family', *The Irish Times*, 11 May 2017.

runs the Knollwood Retirement Community in Washington, DC. Stevie II has the cultured accent of an English gentleman, which is enjoyed by the people who live in that nursing home. Stevie II can also be of assistance to people with disabilities who wish to live alone.[7] At the launch, Dr Conor McGinn said that 'Stevie II embodies a significant technological upgrade and uses advanced AI capabilities so it is considerably more mobile and dextrous than Stevie I.'[8] Stevie II uses advanced sensing technologies which include laser rangefinders, depth cameras and tactile sensors to help it perform various tasks. Dr McGinn said that the creators of Stevie II have 'humanised the technology in a way that surpassed our expectations'.[9]

Dr McGinn is aware of the ethical and psychological issues involved, for example, where elderly people in nursing homes might tend to form a deeper attachment to their robot than to their family or friends. He has seen evidence of this around him. Many people today are addicted to their mobile phones, constantly calling and texting third parties, even while they are having a conversation with another person who is sitting with them. That is why more and more schools are banning the use of mobile phones during school hours.

Dr McGinn sees other ethical issues surrounding this new robotic technology. He believes that if you build realistic, humanlike robots, you are basically deceiving people, and that is unethical.[10]

Ethical Principles

Professor Alan Winfield, Professor of Robot Ethics at the Bristol Robotic Laboratory, has drawn up a list of ethical principles for engineers and programmers who are manufacturing robots that might be used in nursing homes. As an ethicist, he is aware

7 Allison Bray, 'Robo-Carer: AI prototype Stevie 2 could be futuristic friend for elderly', *Irish Independent*, 16 May 2019.

8 Conor Pope 'Cheerful robot caregiver gets review from humans', *The Irish Times*, 16 May 2019.

9 Ibid.

10 Ibid.

of the possible societal, economic and environmental negative consequences of robots on human beings. He cites the example of self-driven cars and makes the point that while the companies that are manufacturing these vehicles may be testing them, there are still no national or international safety standards. According to him, we urgently need such standards, together with new, well-resourced agencies that will certify safety in robots and investigate when problems arise. I will address some of these concerns in Chapter 9.

Professor Alan Winfield is the co-chair of the General Principles Committee at Trinity College, Dublin. This committee is developing ethical principles that will be applied to all AI and autonomous systems, such as self-driven cars, drones, medical diagnosis, and search engines. These principles maintain that such systems should not infringe on a person's human rights and that their functioning should be transparent. Winfield feels that it is vital that ethics should be factored into every aspect of AI and autonomous systems development, right from the very beginning to the end of the design process. He and others are clear that education in ethics is essential for all those who are involved in AI.

Philosophers, theologians, social scientists and the various religions must reflect on the practical impact and applicability of ethics on this new and powerful technology. Overall, Dr Winfield believes robotics and AI have already brought many benefits to humans, such as the assisted living robots that could help the elderly in their homes. The ethical goal for engineers and programmers must be to create robots that benefit humankind and the earth, rather than designing robots that satisfy their own scientific curiosity or their desire to make money.[11]

Winfield would agree with Professor McGinn that a robot should never be designed to deceive. That means that their mechanical nature should be obvious and transparent. For the users, it must

11 Jeremy Allen, 'Alan Winfield – paving the way for ethical robots', UWE University of West England, 19 May 2017 (https://blogs.uwe.ac.uk/research-business-innovation/alan-winfield-paving-the-way-for-ethical-robots/).

be clear that robots are machines, and, even though they are sophisticatedly engineered, that they do not possess human qualities such as understanding, concern and empathy.[12] Trinity is fortunate that in conjunction with ADAPT, Ireland's centre for digital content technology, there is now an MSc studentship in 'Ethics for Artificial Intelligence', where these novel and difficult ethical questions can be explored and resolved. It is also good to see that other Irish universities, such as Dublin City University, University College Dublin and The Dublin Institute of Technology, are also involved with ADAPT in this regard.[13]

Unfortunately, it is often difficult to convince programmers about the importance of including ethical issues. Journalist Rana Foroohar captures this in an article in the *Financial Times* entitled 'Big Tech is cut off from the real world'. She cites the experience of Frank Pasquale, a University of Maryland law professor and a noted critic of big tech. He was describing a conversation he had with a Silicon Valley consultant about the neutrality of a search engine. Pasquale was making the point that search engine owners should not be able to favour their own content. The consultant dismissed this concern with the comment that 'we can't code for that'. Pasquale reminded the consultant that this was a legal issue and not a technical one. The consultant restated his position by saying, 'Yes, but we can't code for it, so it can't be done.' The consultant was stating that all debates would be held on his terms or not at all which is very dangerous.[14]

The '*Waifu*' Robot

The last census in Japan in 2015 showed that one third of Japanese homes are occupied by only one person. This can result in an experience of loneliness for many. One company responding to this widespread experience of loneliness, Gatebox, is creating '*waifu*'

12 Dan Jolin, 'Should A Robot Be Your Child's Best Mate?' *The Observer*, 19 September 2017.
13 Adapt Centre, 'MSc Studentship in Ethics of Artificial Intelligence' (https://www.adaptcentre.ie/about/jobs/msc-studentship-in-ethics-of-artificial-intelligence).
14 Rana Foroohar, 'Big Tech is cut off from the real world', *Financial Times*, 3 July 2017.

robots.[15] Based on 'anime' characters from Japanese pop-culture and targeted exclusively at lonely 'salarymen' the *waifu* robot works in many ways like Alexa and other AI assistants. It will wake up its owner every morning, then it will remind them to bring their equipment, such as a laptop, to work. The *waifu* robot listens to the weather forecast and, if it is raining or threatening to rain, the owner is encouraged to take an umbrella. While the owner is at work, the robot sends affirmative messages and makes sure that the heating is turned on in the house before they arrive home in the evening. When they do, the robot greets them and tells them what is worth watching on TV that evening. Finally, the robot wishes them a good night.

The *waifu* robot is designed exclusively for men and draws on a pre-existing Japanese subculture that encourages the idolising of female anime characters. As was already discussed in relation to Alexa this is problematic because the interaction mirrors the misogynistic bias found in many cultures. Furthermore, a dependent relationship with a robot could make it difficult for people to enter loving and trusting relationships with each other. All relationships will, at times, have disagreements and difficulties. These are a central element in any growing and deepening relationship, and a relationship with a robot can never replicate that.

The Impact of the New Technology on Health

Advances in the clinical use of AI will continue to have a profound effect on medicine and on the global medical workforce. Machine learning has proved to be very effective in scanning diagnostic images in the search for cancerous growths. According to the World Health Organisation (WHO), 400 million people do not have access to the most basic medical services.[16] WHO hopes that AI will make

15 Sean Gallagher, 'The holographic anime "robot" that will keep house for lonely salarymen', *Ars Technica*, 18 December 2016 (https://arstechnica.com/information-technology/2016/12/the-anime-girlfriend-experience-gateboxs-ai-powered-holographic-home-robot/).

16 Richard Vize, 'Technology could redefine the doctor-patient relationship', *The Guardian*, 11 March 2017 (https://www.theguardian.com/healthcare-network/2017/mar/11/artificial-intelligence-nhs-doctor-patient-relationship).

affordable healthcare accessible to all people, not just those who live in wealthy countries. This will not happen without serious financial planning, the availability of functioning internet technology and global political commitment.

In 2019, revolutionary 3D technology brought some significant breakthroughs in the diagnosis of pancreatic cancers. The technique was developed in the Francis Crick Institute in London. 3D imagery showed that pancreatic cancer can start and grow in two distinct ways: this was not known until then. For a long time, researchers were studying two-dimensional slices of the cancer tumour which showed abnormal shapes. This meant that oncologists were in some cases unable to explain what was happening. Now, with this new 3D imagery, doctors were able to distinguish two distinct types of pancreatic cancer formation. One of the cancers grows outwards, while the other grows inwards into the ducts of the pancreas. The two types of cancer are biologically different. Dr Behrens, one of the doctors who worked on the project, said that 'our study revealed pancreatic cancer to have fundamental shapes that are different. You can now understand what people have been seeing in two dimensions for decades.'[17]

AI in Emergency Medicine

Since 2018, when a person calls the emergency services in Denmark, two things happen in tandem. A human voice answers the phone, but an AI assistant also listens to the conversation.[18] This device, which has been developed by Danish start-up company Corti, listens for signs of a potential heart attack as soon as the patient begins talking. The device employs algorithms called neural networks. These consist of many different computation layers which act in a somewhat similar way to neurons that are connected in the human

17 Verity Bowman, '3D; tech delivers leap forward in the treatment of killer cancer', *Irish Independent*, 4 February 2019.

18 Timothy Revell, 'AI can hear a cardiac arrest', *New Scientist*, 13 January 2018.

brain.[19] While the patient who made the call is answering questions about their age, physical and medical condition, the computer is eavesdropping, and uses speech-recognition software to examine the words and the tone of voice that the patient uses to describe what is happening. The computer then issues an observation about the likelihood of a heart attack. In medical trials, this software detected cardiac arrests accurately in 93 per cent of cases. According to a study carried out by the University of Copenhagen, a human health official at the scene will diagnose cardiac arrest failure in just 73 per cent of cases. Furthermore, the computer reaches its conclusions in forty-eight seconds, which is half a minute faster than a human diagnosis.[20] All in all, this device has the potential to reduce fatalities from heart attacks and strokes, both of which are a major cause of death in many developed countries.

AI in Stroke and Spinal Injuries

After serious spinal injury caused by an accident or a stroke, AI can help people regain their mobility. A robot harness now offers individualised treatment that will improve a person's ability to walk again. This is an extraordinary treatment that could not have been envisaged ten or fifteen years ago. Until recently, several physiotherapists would be required to physically support and guide a patient who was learning to walk again.[21] Scientists from the Swiss Federal Institute of Technology in Lausanne have developed a harness that can correct the patient's gait by gently pushing the patient forward or backward or from side to side. This new smart harness, RYSEN, collects information on the movement of the legs, stride patterns and muscle activity from body sensors, and provides assistance that is tailored to the needs of the individual patient. It will measure how much force should be applied to a patient's trunk to produce a natural gait.

19 Ibid.
20 Ibid.
21 Nicole Kobie, 'Robot physio helps people walk again', *New Scientist*, 29 July 2017.

Neuroscientist Grégoire Courtine of the Swiss team, told the *New Scientist* that the algorithm evaluates the optimal amount of body weight support for each patient.[22] In addition, the harness helps the patient recover muscle mass. It also retrains the brain to handle the delicate balance between the pull of gravity, on the one hand, and the forward movement that is required for walking, on the other. When this device comes on the market, it will change the lives of many people who, until now, have lost the ability to walk.

AI in Parkinson's Disease

AI can help people with other diseases as well. A lot of significant research on Parkinson's disease is taking place in NUI Galway's School of Medicine. Many people with Parkinson's suffer from what is called freezing of the gait, where they feel that their feet are glued to the ground. Leo Quinlan, a physiologist who works at NUI Galway, believes that the severity of the freezing of their gait is determined by the stage of the Parkinson's disease that the patient presents with. He and Gearóid Ó Laighin, the Professor of Electronic Engineering, are investigating Parkinson's disease at the Human Movement Laboratory at NUI Galway's Cúram Centre for Research in Medical Devices. The user wears the device, called CueStim, on their waist. This is connected to small electrodes on the skin of their thigh. Rather than sending a signal to stimulate muscle movement, the device uses the skin as a pathway to signal the brain to move out of the 'freezing' mode. As well as reducing the likelihood of a fall, CueStim is also intended to help reduce the amount of medication a patient needs to take for the illness. According to Professor Ó Laighin, 'We are using what is referred to as a user-centred design methodology to ensure that the developed technology meets the needs of the intended users. This involves testing all aspects of the system with the Parkinson's

22 Ibid.

community and seeking their feedback on its usability throughout the design process.'[23]

Can AI Machines Replace Doctors or Surgeons?

AI could also have a profound effect on the work of medical personnel, such as doctors, nurses and surgeons. Some robots are currently performing eye operations that are too delicate for a human surgeon to perform manually.[24] During 2018, in Eindhoven in the Netherlands, twelve participants needed to have a membrane removed from their retina, and this involved cutting several cells that were inhibiting their vision. The delicate operation was performed on six of the patients by highly trained eye surgeons, and the other six had the operation performed by a robot. While all the operations were successful, it was found that a patient who availed of the robotic surgery experienced less damage to blood vessels, especially at the back of the eye.[25] The reason for this is that even the best surgeons do not have perfectly steady hands. In practice, this can lead to slight vibrations of the order of one tenth of a millimetre at the tip of their instruments. Though this is tiny, there are parts of the retina, such as the inner limiting membrane, that are only 0.02mm thick. It would be very difficult for a surgeon to apply the tip of a needle to these parts without causing more serious damage. On the other hand, a surgical robot operates at 0.01mm, making it very useful for undertaking these types of operations in the future.

In 2016, surgical robots were trained to make the micro-scale movements needed for the delicate procedure of cataract operations. These robots are called Axsis, and have been developed by Chris Wagner and his team at Cambridge Consultants in the UK. They

23 'NUI Galway develops novel devices to support people with Parkinson's', *Galway Advertiser*, 28 December 2017 (www.advertiser ie/galway-develop-novel-devices-to-support-people-with-parkinson's).

24 Timothy Revell, 'A robot has performed eye surgery on humans for the first time', *New Scientist*, 18 June 2018 (https://www.newscientist.com/article/2171807-a-robot-has-performed-eye-surgery-on-humans-for-the-first-time).

25 Timothy Revell, 'Robot eye surgeon is steadier than a human', *New Scientist*, 23 June 2018.

can make cuts in the eye more accurately than an eye surgeon. It is suggested that, globally, twenty million people have cataract operations every year. One of the dangers of cataract surgery is that the surgeon can, accidentally, pierce the back of the lens, and this can lead to hazy vision.[26]

Robo-Surgery

The Da Vinci XI robot surgery for prostate cancer was developed at NASA in the US. There are major benefits for the patient as the incisions are minimal when compared with the normal operation. Other benefits are that much less blood is lost, pain is reduced, and the hospital stay is far shorter. The surgeon works in a relaxed position so that the robotic instruments can move with far greater dexterity.

In May 2019, a medical start-up company based in Cambridge, England, claimed success in the first clinical trials using a new generation of surgical robots. These robot assistants are involved in operating on patients with a variety of gynaecological and gastrointestinal problems. Operations have taken place at the Deenanagh Mangeshkar Hospital in Puna, India, using the CMS Surgical's Versius robotic assistants. Dhananjay Kelkar, the surgical team leader, said that the thirty-day follow-up on thirty patients who had experienced keyhole surgery showed that the trials had been very successful. The next clinical trial will involve 250 patients who require a hysterectomy. At present, the surgical robots cost more than one million pounds. However, it is expected that the cost will reduce in the future when most patients will opt for this minimal access surgery.[27]

In Japan in 2017, three major claims were being made for the clinical power of AI. IBM's Watson supercomputer was credited with diagnosing in minutes the precise condition affecting a leukaemia

26 Sally Adee, 'Eye, robot', *New Scientist*, 12 November 2016.
27 Clive Cookson, 'Surgical robots trial claims success', *Financial Times*, 14 May 2019.

patient, which had baffled doctors for months. The supercomputer could cross-reference the person's medical records with a database of twenty million oncology records. The computer can store more information than any doctor, and can access this almost instantly. Additionally, it can also benefit from its own past mistakes so that its diagnosis will be more accurate in the future.[28] However, data protection will need to be updated to allow for these procedures to take place.

At Dublin City University (DCU), a start-up company, Deciphex, has developed a solution to speed up the throughput in diagnosing cancer in busy pathology departments, by using a combination of AI and computer-based diagnostics. The founders of the company were aware that in most other diagnostic areas, such as MRI and CT scanning, the results can be read on a screen. In pathology, on the other hand, the current processes are still manual. The first stage is for a laboratory technician to prepare a slide or microbiological culture, and then place it under a microscope to be analysed by a pathologist. One can imagine the pressure that this places on overloaded pathology departments that are attempting to get results quickly for doctors and, more importantly, for patients. Deciphex uses AI and diagnostics to enable the pathologists to read the results on a monitor, rather than under a microscope. This digital pathology uses AI and deep-learning to examine tissues from biopsies, which, of course, speeds up the process and improve clinical accuracy, both of which benefit the pathology department and the patient. Donal O'Shea, one of the founders of the company, points out that across the world, it would cost about $12 billion to employ pathologists to diagnose various diseases. Already, there is great interest in both Britain and the US in Deciphex's solutions.[29]

When the outbreak of Covid-19 began in Wuhan in China in

28 'IBM's Watson: Best Doctor in the World', *World Health.Net*, 12 July 2017 (https://www.worldhealth.net/news/ibm-watson-supercomputer-best-doctor-world/).
29 Olive Keogh, 'Progressing pathology to diagnose disease faster', *The Irish Times*, 15 November 2018.

2019 a new hospital ward was built for those who contracted the coronavirus. This was the first hospital run entirely by robots. As a way to protect the nursing, medical and cleaning staff, robots brought food, liquids and medicine to the Covid-19 patients. At the moment in China, the robots look after people who are not acutely ill. When patients get better, they are allowed to go home. If the patient's condition becomes more critical, they are transferred to a ward run by humans.

In that hospital, people were quite aware of the dangers of contracting the virus, as the hospital's director, Liu Zhiming, died of the disease in March 2020. In the ward, various types of robots moved around autonomously, but they were under the control of nursing and medical staff outside the ward. This trial was a cooperative venture involving a Beijing-based robot company, China Mobile and Wuchang in Wuhan.

The Future

At the June 2018 Digital Health London Summit, Ali Parsa, founder of digital healthcare company Babylon, argued that mobile technology, coupled with AI, could make universal healthcare available to people globally, partly by replacing doctors with AI systems, which will cut costs. He claimed that there will not be any solution to hospital overcrowding if we rely on humans alone. The use of AI and modern technologies will be essential to the provision of good and competent medical services for everyone. Ali Parsa believes that this AI will have a major impact on medical personnel, by augmenting the pool of medical talent available, and also by replacing medical staff. But, as noted about teachers in the previous chapter, doctors and other healthcare professionals will still have a central role, even in the era of these new technologies.

Conclusion

In this chapter, we have seen that AI is already having a major impact on all aspects of healthcare. AI devices are being used in many locations, especially in Japan, in caring for elderly people and for the young. Other robotic devices give independence to people who are suffering from various diseases. Right across the medical world, AI is already helping patients by diagnosing their diseases, often much more quickly than doctors have done in the past. AI has also been used in the area of surgery, and it can perform many operations that are much less invasive than those traditionally performed by surgeons. The Da Vinci XI robotic surgery for prostate cancer is a good example of what is currently happening, as is the technology for delicate eye operations. The one thing we can be sure of is that this technology will grow and bring more and more AI into medicine over the next decade or two. Some commentators are now speculating that these new technologies will reduce the number of health and care workers in the future.

Chapter 7
The Impact of AI on Retail, Hospitality, Banking, Finance and Call Centres

Retail outlets selling a variety of goods have been part of our culture for many generations. In the 1940s, 1950s and 1960s, different shops specialised in providing a particular range of products. Some sold food exclusively, while others sold clothing and footwear. Hardware stores sold electrical supplies, plumbing equipment and home improvement materials, and pharmacists sold medicine and medical devices. Most of the shops were family-run businesses, and employed both family members and local people. From the end of the 1960s onwards, foreign and local supermarkets and chain stores moved into the retail trade.

In many ways, the experience of shopping changed with the arrival of the supermarkets and chain stores. Most of the employees now work at either the checkout desks or at restocking items on the shop shelves. Unfortunately, the jobs of both groups are under threat from technology.

Cashless Stores

In recent years, supermarkets have further down-sized their staff numbers by installing self-checkout desks. In an era of drones, robots and increased AI, Amazon's decision to open a cashier-less convenience store is unsurprising. The first such store was opened by Amazon in Seattle on 22 January 2018, and featured on news channels around the world. Amazon chose to use machine learning, computer vision and AI to ensure that there would be no queues at the checkout desks. To shop at the store, customers must download the Amazon Go app, and then scan their own unique code to gain entry.[1] Once inside the store, shoppers can take anything they want from the shelves, and the cost will be charged to their card. If customers change their minds and decide not to take an item, the price will be automatically credited to the card once the item is replaced on the shelf. This new technology is now available in many shops across the world. Gaby Hinsliff of *The Guardian* thought it was ironic that while everyone was praising supermarket workers during the Covid-19 pandemic, the public address systems inside some of the stores were encouraging shoppers to download the self-scanning app. This would mean they would not have to go through the checkout. Consequently, cashiers will lose their jobs.[2] Those who have worked tirelessly to restock the stores' shelves during the pandemic will also be made redundant by automation, which was already rippling beneath the surface before the pandemic struck.

Online Sales

Amazon has profited greatly from its retail model. Jeff Bezos, founder and chief executive of Amazon, is the world's richest businessman. He has done well economically during the Covid-19 crisis. Since many people were using Amazon to order online, this boosted Bezos's fortune by $30 billion.[3] He is now on course to become the world's first trillionaire. However, while he is doing well, not all his employees are as lucky. Tim Bray, vice-president of Amazon's cloud computing arm, announced that he had resigned in dismay over the firings of workers who had raised queries about workplace safety during the pandemic.[4]

Some politicians, such as Senator Bernie Sanders in the US,

1 'Retail in the Age of Amazon', Posted in: *Business, Commercial Real Estate, Real Estate Technology*, 18 January 2018 (http://backventures.com/retail-in-the-age-of-amazon).

2 Gaby Hinsliff, 'New technologies tend to be difficult to implement. Unfortunately, for many workers, difficult is the new normal', *The Guardian*, 30 April 2020 (https://www.theguardian.com/commentisfree/2020/apr/30/coronavirus-disruption-automation).

3 Kathy Sheridan, 'Hard to socially distance from Amazon', *The Irish Times*, 20 May 2020 (http://www.irishtimes.com/opinion/fathy-seridan-hard-to-socially-diastance-from-amazon-1.4257418).

4 Ibid.

have been very critical of the poor pay and conditions of Amazon's warehouse workers. Unless Amazon changes these practices, Sanders is proposing to introduce a bill to tax companies that do not pay their workers a decent living wage. Amazon's workers often have to use food stamps and other public assistance in order to make ends meet. In Britain, Amazon's pay and work practices have been criticised by trade unionists, politicians and religious leaders. In October 2018, the Archbishop of Canterbury, Justin Welby, criticised Amazon for not paying workers a living wage. He also said that Amazon was 'leeching off the taxpayer by paying too little tax'.[5]

Amazon increased the minimum wage of employees in the US to $15 an hour in November 2018. In Britain, Amazon's 40,000 permanent and temporary staff also got a wage increase, bringing their pay to £10.50 an hour in London, and £9.50 across the rest of the UK. This wage increase came into force in November 2018.[6]

The impact of online selling can be seen by the Marks & Spencer announcement in March 2019 of their plans to cut ninety-seven jobs in Ireland. More job losses are also predicted in the retail trade as employers opt for self-service checkouts and online shopping. Even the unions can do little to stop this trend. Gerry Light, from the Mandate Union, says that nobody knows how many jobs will be lost in the future, since retail is already being impacted by technology.[7]

Online shopping, in general, is putting huge pressure on traditional shops. In July 2018, the House of Fraser prepared to close half of its shops in Britain and to cut 11,000 jobs because its retail business was contracting.[8] Alex Williamson, the chief executive, was clear that unless he intervened with his plans to cut

5 Ibid.

6 Richard Partington, 'Amazon raises minimum wage for US and UK employees', *The Guardian*, 2 October 2018 (https://www.theguardian.com/technology/2018/oct/02/amazon-raises-minimum-wage-us-uk-employees).

7 Anne-Marie Walsh, 'M&S to cut jobs as union warns of automated check-out threat', *Irish Independent*, 21 March 2019.

8 Sarah Butler and Zoe Wood, 'Failing high street chains leave 11,000 more jobs under threat', *The Guardian*, 8 June 2018.

jobs, the whole business was likely to collapse.[9] The House of Fraser is not the only high-street business in Britain to be on the verge of collapse. In 2018, Debenhams, one of Britain's best-known brands, found that its 2018 valuation had fallen by an astonishing 95 per cent since it was floated on the stock market in 2006. Spanish/Swiss businessman Sergio Rodriguez Bucher, who became the chief executive of Debenhams in October 2016, blamed a challenging environment for the crash. According to him, consumers were not spending much money at the time, and much of what they were spending was online.[10] His time at the Debenhams' helm was not very successful, and he resigned in April 2019.[11]

In April 2020, Debenhams confirmed that it intended to put its UK business into administration to counteract possible legal action that could force it into liquidation. In Ireland, the company informed its 2,000 staff that it was going into liquidation, and that it would not be opening after the Covid-19 emergency. Effectively, all of those jobs are gone. Auditors Kieran Wallace and Andrew O'Leary from the firm KPMG were appointed liquidators of Debenhams Retail Ireland in April 2020.

Will Covid-19 Kill off the US Department Store?

In the spring of 2020, the retail trade in the US was also under pressure. In October 2018, Sears, the 125-year-old US department store, filed for a Chapter 11 bankruptcy protection. This bankruptcy route in the US allows businesses with heavy debts to reorganise their business. In this case, it allowed Sears to cut its debts and keep operating, at least through the Christmas holiday period. Sears was the traditional department store, selling everything to everyone, everywhere in the US. In recent years, it was overtaken by Walmart

9 Ibid.

10 Ben Chapman, 'What went wrong for Debenhams and how can the department store chain turn things around?' *The Independent*, 11 September, 2018 (https://www.independent.co.uk/news/business/analysis-and-features/debenhams-what-went-wrong-sales-down-share-price-department-store-chain-a8531726.html).

11 Anne-Marie Walsh, 'Debenhams closure puts 1,600 Irish Jobs at risk', *Irish Independent*, 16 January 2019.

and Home Depot and, of course, Amazon. Over the past five years, Sears has lost a staggering $5.8 billion. A decade ago, it employed 302,000 people. However, by 2018, Sears and Kmart (the big box department chain store that bought Sears in 2004) combined employed only 68,000 people. The company has $11.3 billion in liabilities and $7 billion in assets. It is planning to close 142 more stores as it tries to reduce costs and find a way forward.[12]

In December 2017, *The Guardian* reported that a string of retailers and restaurant groups, including Mothercare, Carpetright, New Look, Prezzo and Jamie's Italian, were planning to close hundreds of outlets.

In order to save jobs in high street stores, people like Mike Ashley, founder and chief executive of Sports Direct, are calling for a tax on retailers who market more than a fifth of their sales online. He believes that the internet is killing the high street.[13] One thing that seems clear is that high street stores will not employ huge numbers of store assistants in the future. According to the annual report of real estate adviser Altus Group, published in January 2019, 23,000 shops were forecast to close in 2019, mainly because of pressure from online shopping. A further 175,000 jobs will be shed from struggling shops on the high street.[14]

A headline in *The New York Times* on 21 April 2020 proclaims boldly that Covid-19 will cause the demise of the department store right across the US and that very few are likely to survive.[15] This has already begun to happen among luxury retailers. Neiman Marcus

12 Michael Corkery, 'Sears, the Original Everything Store, Files for Bankruptcy', *The New York Times*, 14 October 2018 (https://www.nytimes.com/2018/10/14/business/sears-bankruptcy-filing-chapter-11.html).

13 Sarah Butler, 'Tax online sales to save high streets, Ashley tells MPs', *The Guardian*, 4 December 2018.

14 Rebecca Smithers, 'Over 23,000 shops and 175,000 high street jobs predicted to go in 2019', *The Guardian*, 20 January 2019.

15 Sapna Maheshwari and Vanessa Friedman, 'The Death of the Department Store: Very Few Are Likely to Survive', *The New York Times*, 21 April 2020 (https://www.nytimes.com/2020/04/21/business/coronavirus-department-stores-neiman marcus.html?campaign_id=2&emc=edit_th_200422&instance_id=17813&nl=todaysheadlines®i_id=67440878&segment_id=25708&user_id=7f727204d4655138e2edeeed5475da14).

Group has filed for bankruptcy. Unfortunately, it will not be the only retailer forced to close permanently. Like other commentators, Mark A. Cohen, Director of Retail Studies at Columbia University's Business School, believes that major problems with department stores have been there for a number of years, due to online shopping. In 2020, at the time of the spring sales, when revenues should be soaring, stores were furloughing tens of thousands of corporate and store employees, hoarding cash and planning desperately to survive the Covid-19 crisis.[16] JC Penney, the budget-friendly family clothing and home furnishings store, which had been in decline for twenty years, became a victim of Covid-19. As a result, it filed for bankruptcy on 15 May 2020. Many will agree that when a shopping chain like JC Penney closes its shops in malls, this will have major implications for mall landscapes across the US.[17]

Covid-19 undermined one of the main attractions of shopping in a retail store. Social distancing of two metres meant that a shopper often had to wait outside the store until those who were inside the store had completed their business. A person could envisage doing this during the fine weather of April or May, but not during the dark, cold wet days of November or December. Another advantage of traditional shopping is that one could try on clothes before buying them. With the Covid-19 pandemic, shoppers cannot touch any of the clothes in the shop because of the fear that they might pass on the virus. We are being told that this is the new normal, at least until a vaccine is discovered.

AI in the Hospitality Industry

The first fully-automated restaurant, Eatsa, opened in San Francisco in 2016. Customers' meals are served approximately ninety seconds after the order is made and paid for on a wall-mounted electronic

16 Ibid.

17 Sapna Maheshwari and Michael Corkery, 'J.C. Penney, 118-Year-Old Department Store, Files for Bankruptcy', *The New York Times*, 15 May 2020 (https://www.nytimes.com/2020/05/15/business/jc-penney-bankruptcy-coronavirus.html?action=click&module=Top%20Stories&pgtype=Homepage).

tablet. Though it appears that there are no waiters or cashiers, the company admits it has a small kitchen staff, and one employee in the front of the house answers questions about how to order the food.[18] The restaurant appears to be doing well, and the owners have opened another branch in Los Angeles. Similar robot restaurants have opened in New York, Bangkok, Japan, Korea and China. If this development continues, it will have a serious effect on employment in restaurants. Millions of people, including students, who work part-time as waiters or waitresses, will be affected. In the past, students could help subsidise their education costs with restaurant work. Before the Covid-19 pandemic, more than 2.3 million people were working in restaurants across the US.[19] As fully automated restaurants are rolled out, some people fear that these jobs will disappear.

There are Limits to What Robots Can Do

A high-tech hotel in Japan has been forced to lay off half of its robot staff after finding that they were incompetent and created more work for humans. At the Henn na Hotel in Tokyo the robots were introduced partly as a novelty, and partly to reduce the need for human staff and to lower costs.[20] The hotel started with eighty robots, but the number quickly increased to 243. The hotel website boasted that it was the first hotel in the world staffed by robots. However, the robotic concierges were unable to answer simple questions from the guests when they were checking in or checking out. Even when the guests were in their rooms, the actions of the robots were annoying. The egg-shaped robot, named Churi, was criticised by many guests for chiming in with standard responses,

18 Julia Carrie Wong, 'Welcome to the robot-based workforce: will your job become automated too?' *The Observer*, 19 March 2016 (https://www.theguardian.com/technology/2016/mar/19/robot-based-economy-san-francisco).

19 Alec Ross, *The Industries of the Future*, London: Simon & Schuster, 2016, 39.

20 'Hotel sacks half of its robot staff for being bad at their jobs', *Irish Independent*, 19 January 2019 (https://www.independent.ie/world-news/asia-pacific/hotel-sacks-half-of-its-robot-staff-for-being-bad-at-their-jobs-37727564.html).

'Sorry, I couldn't catch that? Could you repeat your request?' These answers were often given by the robots, not to genuine questions from the guests, but, for example, if guests were snoring during the night.[21] In a world where workers are increasingly worried that their jobs will be automated, this robot hotel experience appears to tell us that humans like to interact with other human beings. Once the novelty of robotic workers fades, it seems that people will still want to be served by other human beings, especially in the hospitality business.

How AI Affects Employment

Until very recently, it was assumed that, if a person had a good education and was willing to work hard, it would be easy to get a permanent job. With the rise of robots, AI and 'big' data, that concept is certainly beginning to crumble. In Ireland, before the Covid-19 crisis, many people, including politicians, still viewed full employment as the way forward for the country economically. In September 2018, the Central Statistics Office (CSO) stated that the unemployment rate in the Republic of Ireland had dropped from 16 per cent in 2011 to 5.1 per cent in 2018. This was the lowest unemployment rate since 2006.[22] All that changed with the arrival of the Covid-19 pandemic in 2020. Unemployment has now skyrocketed in almost every country in the world, and unemployment among young people is particularly high.

The International Monetary Fund (IMF) also seemed to be blind to the impact of AI and automation on jobs. Following the financial crash in 2008, Christine Lagarde, then chief executive of the IMF, praised Ireland for the remarkable recovery it had made between 2015 to 2019. Even though she discussed possible difficulties for the Irish economy such as Brexit and a global trade war, she did not mention the effect that new technologies were

21 Ibid.

22 Eoin Burke-Kennedy, 'Jobless rate hits new post-crash low of 5.1%', *The Irish Times*, 4 July 2018.

having on jobs. She maintained that the state must ensure it has the resources, the rainy-day funds, and a stable fiscal position to resist potential shocks, such as Brexit.[23]

In the US, despite threats of a major trade war with China and Europe, the economy was strong before the Covid-19 pandemic changed the economic situation. Six hundred thousand people had joined the work force in June 2018, according to figures in the monthly report published by the Labour Department on 6 July of that year.[24]The number of people working part-time because of their inability to find a full-time job also fell. Though the unemployment rate was at 4 per cent, Catherine Barrera, chief economist of the online job site, ZipRecuiter, was not concerned. According to her, there were still some people who were not participating in the labour force at that time, and they needed to be encouraged to return to work.[25] Clearly, the view was that the US was close to full employment, but now all that has changed.

In the UK, unemployment rates fell from 7.7 per cent in 2013 to 4.4 per cent in August 2017. In 2018, then British Prime Minister Theresa May also seemed to envisage full employment as the norm in Britain. In a speech at the Conservative Party conference in September 2016, she declared that 'We are building a new centre ground in British politics – and improving the pay, security and rights of ordinary working people, which is a key part of building a country and an economy that works for everyone, not just the privileged few.'[26] Once again, there was no mention of the impact of automation on jobs that will be lost in the next two decades.

The Joseph Rowntree Foundation is an independent organisation

23 Harry McGee, 'IMF head Christine Lagarde praises Ireland's economy', *The Irish Times*, 25 June 2018 (https://www.irishtimes.com/news/politics/imf-head-christine-lagarde-praises-ireland-s-economy-1.3542993).

24 Patricia Cohen, 'Employers' Hiring Push Brings Workers Off the Bench', *The New York Times*, 6 July, 2018 (https://www.nytimes.com/2018/07/06/business/economy/jobs-report.html?emc=edit_na_20180706&nl=breaking-news&nlid=67440878ing-news&ref=cta).

25 Ibid.

26 Lynn Davidson, 'Job Rights Revolution, PM Theresa May pledges to protect workers' rights for those "just managing" to get by', *The Sun*, 1 October 2016.

working to inspire social change through research and policy making. A study by this organisation shows that more than half a million British workers fell into poverty between 2014 and 2017. It also found that the actual number of workers living in poverty reached four million. This means that one in eight people in Britain are now classified as working poor because of low wages, an erosion of welfare and the rising cost of living.[27]

Jobs in The Financial Sector

Writing in the *New Scientist* in October 2017, Sally Adee drew attention to the fact that the financial markets are now dominated by robots and AI. She quotes Andrew Lo, Professor of Finance at the Massachusetts Institute of Technology (MIT), who has studied the speed at which the financial sector is changing. He says that AI technology has completely transformed the financial system. Most of the day-to-day trading is done purely algorithmically.[28] However, some of the technology, which reduces costs to investors, increases market volatility. This enables trading firms to profit at the expense of the individual. Companies use sophisticated software to trade shares in one-millionth of a second. Elaine Moore is deputy editor of the *Financial Times* and regularly comments on the technology industry. In 2013, she stated that half of the trade on the US equity market and approximately a third of the trade in Europe is done by algorithms. This means that human beings are increasingly sidelined when it comes to buying and selling shares.[29]

Peter Randall, who helped to develop Chi-X Europe into Europe's largest share trading platform, feels that the role of humans in the markets today is like a pilot in a modern aircraft.

27 Richard Partington, 'Steep rise in working families living below the breadline, report finds', *The Guardian*, 4 December 2018.

28 Sally Adee, 'The money machine,' *New Scientist*, 14 October 2017 (https://www.newscientist.com/article/mg23631470-100-the-stock-market-is-run-by-wild-robots-we-dont-fully-control/).

29 Elaine Moore, 'Humans or machines: who's running the markets?' *Financial Times*, 15 March 2013.

The aircraft uses computers to take off, fly the plane and land safely at airports, but if something goes wrong, it is essential that the pilot is there to sort out the problem.[30]

How many humans will be involved in financial trading in the future? In 2020, it is obvious that many traders are losing their jobs. The transformation of the financial markets has happened so suddenly that few people are aware that it is happening.[31] In recent years, banks and investment funds have been rolling out machine-learning to suggest what might be the best price to buy or sell stocks. US billionaire hedge fund manager Steven Cohen is considering replacing many of his top money managers with AI machines. More worrying still in terms of job losses, is the belief of venture capitalist Marc Andreessen that 100,000 financial workers are not needed to keep money flowing.[32]

Something similar is happening at Optimas, a prestigious Boston-based consultancy firm. The firm warned its workers in 2017 that more than 90,000 jobs in the asset management industry could be lost because of the rise of AI. The company claimed that the asset management industry would be more affected than other elements of the financial services business. The company's chief executive, Octavio Marenzi, said that AI will lead to job cuts in the back office, operational systems and customer service.[33]

Investment banks are also trying to use AI, automation and robots to help them cut costs. In August 2018, JP Morgan announced that it would soon use a first-of-its-kind robot to execute trades across its global equities' business. This was after a European trial of the bank's new AI programme showed it was more efficient than traditional methods of buying and selling shares.[34]

30 Ibid.
31 Ibid.
32 Saijel Kishan, Hugh Son and Mira Rojanaskul, 'Robots are coming for these Wall Street Jobs', Bloomberg, 18 October 2017 (https://www.bloomberg.com/graphics/2017-wall-street-robots/)
33 Madison Marriage, 'Fund managers deny AI threatens jobs', *Financial Times*, 14 August 2017.
34 Laura Noonan, 'Algorithms robot to help JP Morgan execute trades', *Financial Times*, 1 August 2017.

A hedge fund is an investment fund that pools capital from accredited individuals and institutional investors, and invests in a variety of assets. Worldwide, around 9,000 hedge funds are active and open for investment, and algorithms are actively searching the markets for patterns that might yield a competitive edge. According to Andrew Lo, the symbiosis between technology and finance has accelerated the pace of the financial markets beyond human capacity at all levels of the financial system.[35] Lo believes that we don't understand the financial network. Naturally, people fear that because everything is interconnected, a financial crash could start anywhere in the world and affect everyone. Consequently, there is quite a lot of fear in the financial sector.

Banking Systems

AI technology is already being used in customer service in banks. The Japanese bank, SoftBank, replaced staff at its Tokyo branch with ten 'Pepper' robots. Pepper answers questions, offers suggestions and interacts with customers by responding to their tone of voice and facial expressions.[36] Pepper can carry out these complex tasks, and is also continually learning how to do things better and faster. This trend is not confined to Japan. John Cryan, the chief executive of Deutsche Bank, issued a stark warning to his staff in September 2017, when he said that a big number of his financial analysts will lose their jobs as robots take over.[37] He went on to say that 'We have people behaving like robots. Tomorrow we will have robots behaving like people.'[38] Lex Sokolin, Global Director at Fintech Strategy for Autonomous Research, predicts that banking and lending could see the bigger changes, with 1.2 million jobs being lost, and potential savings of $450 billion worldwide for the industry. Jobs in the

35 Ibid.
36 Ibid.
37 Jill Treanor and Julia Kollewe, 'Robots will wipe out many banking jobs', *The Guardian*, 7 September 2017.
38 Ibid.

insurance industry will also be affected. Sokolin predicts a loss of 865,000 jobs and a projected $400 billion in savings. Finally, there are 460,000 jobs at risk in the investment management sector.[39]

Nowadays, many companies are hiring mathematicians to improve their algorithms. A Scottish financial hedge fund company based in Edinburgh promises to hire more mathematicians, as they play a crucial role in the development of algorithms that will improve the investment performance.[40] Others feel that although some tasks have been automated in recent years, as AI removes some jobs, it also creates new work.[41] However, the question is whether or not there will be enough jobs for all those seeking employment. Job advertisements for people in the financial sector, including data scientists and people with machine-learning and AI skills, have more than trebled since 2018.[42] Many believe that, in the future, these professionals will be employed in investment teams, where humans and AI will work together.

Accounting

One of the biggest advantages of AI technology is its ability to carry out astonishing calculations. In accounting, the biggest benefit of Robot Process Automation (RPA) is that it can complete repetitive tasks more quickly and more accurately than humans can. RPA is ideal for sifting through and finding patterns in huge amounts of information, such as bank reconciliations. In fact, for management accountants who are accustomed to manually preparing monthly reports that are often out of date before they are printed, these specialist finance robots are very welcome. Prior to RPA, accountants had to match transactions manually, note discrepancies and create journal entries. With the use of robotic-accountants, human

39 Ainsley O'Connell Harris, 'AI Could Kill 2.5 Million Financial Jobs – And Save Banks $1 Trillion', *Autonomous*, 8 May 2018 (https://www.fastcompany.com/40568069/ai-could-kill-2-5-million-financial-jobs-and-save-banks-1-trillion).

40 Ibid.

41 Ibid.

42 Ibid.

accountants can instead focus on investigating and clearing up the discrepancies that the RPA tool discovers. Management accountants will have the time to work on strategy and decision-making, instead of having to spend many hours on manual tasks.

For large and small businesses, robots are engaged in Continuous Accounting. This is an approach to managing the accounting cycle that can be the key to achieving a more strategic finance and accounting function in a business. The system delivers meaningful financial data, in real time, each day. Corporations need this new knowledge in order to compete in an increasingly unknown and fickle global economy. Data is available as it is required, instead of once every three months. As such, Continuous Accounting provides accountants with the means and systems finally to move away from the traditional methods of accounting.[43]

Despite this, it is still important to remember that humans are an integral part of robotic accountancy. Their judgements and nuanced human thinking are critical in directing and growing a business. This combination enables humans and robots to work together to solve problems, as in the fields of education and medicine.

Legal Practice

A new technology-focused legal firm, LexTeck, was launched in Dublin in March 2019. The company is 'streamlining' legal and regulatory administration in business, through digitisation, automation and data capture. According to Larry Fenelon, co-founder and partner in Leman Solicitors, Dublin, at least 40 per cent of existing legal jobs are now vulnerable to automation.[44]

In the US, Steve Lohr has reported on technology, business and economics for *The New York Times* for over two decades. In March

43 Isaac Tucker, 'The Blueprint for Continuous Accounting', *Strategic Finance*, 1 May 2017 (http://sfmagazine.com/post-entry/may-2017-the-blueprint-for-continuous-accounting).
44 Murray Kerchavel, 'Dublin startup out to replace lawyers with software services', *Irish Independent*, 28 March 2019.

2017, he reported that AI was carrying out legal work.[45] Dana Remus, Professor at the University of North Carolina School of Law, and Frank Levy, a labour economist at the Massachusetts Institute of Technology, studied the automation threat to the jobs of lawyers in large law firms. They estimate that if all the new technologies were being used, this would mean an estimated decline of about 13 per cent in lawyers' working hours.

In January 2017, a McKinsey Global Institute study found that while nearly half of all tasks could be partially automated with current technology, only 5 per cent of jobs could be entirely automated. Applying its definition to current technology that is widely available or, at least, being tested in laboratories, McKinsey' Global Institute estimates that 23 per cent of a lawyer's work can be automated. Many of the tasks that will be assigned to AI will be of the search-and-find type.[46] One of these might be studying past court decisions and filing the data to make profiles and predictions about how a judge might decide on a current case.

The McKinsey study predicts that highly paid lawyers will concentrate their time and energy on work at the upper end of the legal scale. Other legal services will be performed by non-lawyer assistants.[47] One lawyer, Mr Toon, made the point that the bulk of his time involves devising strategies, thinking creatively and showing empathy to his clients. While he is convinced that these qualities cannot be automated, it is possible that a lot of traditional jobs will be lost in that sector.

The Effects of AI on Jobs in the Public Sector

AI and automation will also affect jobs in the public sector. Reform, a British think tank based in London, was established to seek a

45 Steve Lohr, 'A.I. is Doing Legal Work. But it Won't Replace Lawyers, Yet', *The New York Times*, 19 March 2017 (https://www.nytimes.com/2017/03/19/technology/lawyers-artificial-intelligence.html).
46 Ibid.
47 Ibid.

better way of delivering public services. It believes that AI 'chat-bots' could replace up to 90 per cent of Her Majesty's Civil Service at Whitehall, London. The report argues that the public service is poised to become more flexible as a result of increased numbers embracing the gig economy and working from home, as happened during the Covid-19 pandemic in 2020. In that scenario, workers would support themselves through a variety of flexible jobs, acquired through online platforms. The think tank also believes that tens of thousands of National Health Service (NHS) personnel and GP surgery staff could be replaced by robots by 2030. This would mean a saving of as much as £4 billion a year for the exchequer.[48]

Alexander Hitchcock, the co-author of the report, believes that such a rapid advance in the use of technology may seem controversial, and job losses must be handled sensitively.[49] It might, however, run into strong opposition from unions and the public, especially in the wake of the Covid-19 pandemic, when the hands-on presence of nursing and medical staff was seen as crucial to those who fell ill.

AI in Call Centres

At Google's 2010 annual development conference in California, the company launched Google Assistant. This piece of software allowed a virtual assistant to speak so fluently that most people believed it was a human voice. Scott Huffman, a software engineer at Google, pointed out that until then, creating a new voice took hundreds of hours in a recording studio.[50] With the development of this new technology and the accompanying advances in AI, new voices can be created in just a few weeks. These voices are able to capture subtleties such as pitch, pace and pauses, so that they can convey the same meaning as natural voices.[51]

48 Damien Gayle, 'Almost 250,000 public sector workers could lose their jobs to robots in the next 15 years', *The Guardian*, 6 February 2017 (https://enlight.tech/2017/05/31/smart-artificial-intelligence-will-change-home-automation).

49 Ibid.

50 Ibid.

51 Zoe Wood, 'How rise of robot technology threatens to terminate the British call-centre workforce', *The Observer*, 13 May 2018.

In April 2028, *Observer* journalist Zoe Wood reported that Virgin Media surprised many people by closing their call centre in Swansea, Wales, with the loss of 800 jobs.[52] In the UK in 2018, approximately 6,200 customer service centres employed nearly 1.3 million people.

The demise of call centres would also be disastrous for the Philippine economy. An article on call centres in the *Economist* in 2016 confirmed that the Philippine economy has been transformed by call-centre technology.[53] Call centres began to appear in the Philippines in the 1990s. By 2016, the industry employed 1.2 million people, and their wages accounted for 8 per cent of GDP. The growth of call centres in the past two decades has been a huge benefit for Filipinos who are fluent in English. The development of Google's virtual assistant will lead to wide-scale automation in these call centres, and this will mean fewer jobs. It is predicted that 80 per cent of all call-centre jobs will disappear by 2025. With an average salary of $450 per month, $5.2 billion will disappear from the Philippine economy when these centres close. What industry will replace all of these jobs?[54]

Conclusion

One of the major questions I raise in this book is whether or not these new technologies will lead to mass unemployment, as predicted by Carl Frey and Michael Osborne in their 2013 Oxford study, which asserted that as computerisation enters the more cognitive domain, it will increasingly challenge the old paradigm that new technologies open new markets and provide new jobs. However, in the retail, finance, insurance and call-centre industries, these new technologies are closing down jobs rather than creating them.

52 Ibid.
53 'The end of the line', *The Economist*, 6 February 2016 (https://www.economist.com/news/international/21690041-call-centres-have-created-millions-good-jobs-emerging-world-technology-threatens).
54 Philippine One Outreach, 'The End of Call Centres Will Devastate Manila and Philippines', 13 November 2017 (https://philippineone.com/the-end-of-call-centres-will-devastate-manila-and-philippines).

Chapter 8
Self-driven Cars and Trucks

For the past number of years, car manufacturers around the world have been developing cars that drive themselves. One of the arguments in favour of this is that autonomous cars and trucks are safer and, therefore, road deaths and injuries will be reduced. Most road accidents are caused by human carelessness or the misuse of alcohol and drugs. In 2013, motor vehicles killed around 1.3 million people globally and injured another 50 million. The challenge facing those who are designing self-driven cars is not to build a perfect system, just one that is better than the one we have now.[1] Sebastien Thur is Google's chief engineer in charge of its search for self-driven cars. Much of his motivation to develop safe self-driven cars comes from the fact that his best friend was killed in a car accident.[2]

Experiments with autonomous cars are taking place in the US, China, Japan, Germany, France, Britain and Singapore. In November 2018, the British government announced that self-driven public transport will be functioning on Britain's roads by 2021. Business Secretary Greg Clark did not have any doubts when he said that 'the autonomous vehicle will not only revolutionise how we travel, it will improve transport services for those who struggle to access private and public transport'.[3] Clark promised that 25 million pounds would be made available to companies that are developing autonomous vehicles.

1 Sandy Ogn, 'To do the right thing, autonomous cars need to be programmed with human ethics. But how do we get started?' *New Scientist*, 17 January 2017.
2 Alec Ross, *The Industries of the Future*, London: Simon & Schuster, 2016, 29.
3 Chengcheng, 'Robot taxis set to hit roads in London and Edinburgh', *News Europe*, 12 December 2018 (http://www.xinhuanet.com/english/2018-11/23/c_137625247. htm).

Tesla Motors and Autonomous Cars

Tesla Motors, Inc. is an American automobile and energy firm that designs, manufactures and sells electric cars. Elon Musk, the chief executive, claims that his electric cars are cleaner, safer and more innovative than the models made by other automobile companies.[4] In June 2017, an automobile accident occurred at Williston, Florida, when driver Joshua Brown put his Model S into Tesla's autopilot mode and began watching a Harry Potter movie. He crashed into a lorry and was killed. Tesla claims that the car's sensor system failed to recognise a large eighteen-wheeled white truck because the bright sunlight impeded the sensors.

After the crash, Elon Musk tweeted his condolences to the Brown family on their 'tragic' loss. The tweet went on to make the point that this was the first fatal accident in the 130 million miles driven by autonomous vehicles.

This debate about the ethics of using self-driven cars surfaced again in March 2018, when a self-driven car killed a pedestrian, Elaine Herzberg, who was pushing a bicycle across a four-lane highway in Tempe, Arizona. She was struck by an Uber taxi which, at the time, was operating in self-driven mode, even though there was a human driver sitting in the driver's seat.[5] Uber was not deemed responsible for the crash. Yavapai County attorney, Sheila Sullivan Polk, stated in a letter in April 2019 that, 'after a very thorough review of all the evidence ... there is no basis for criminal liability for the Uber corporation'.[6]

Ethics and Self-driven Cars

New rules about regulating self-driven cars will have to confront the ethical question as to who is liable and responsible when a

4 Bill Vlasic, 'A Fatality Forces Tesla to Confront Its Limits', *The New York Times*, 2 July 2016 (http://www.nytimes.com/2016/07/02/business/a-fatality-forces-tesla-to-confront-its-limits.html?ref=business).

5 Douglas Heaven, 'Robot laws', *New Scientist*, 4 August 2018.

6 Neil Briscoe, 'Who's to blame when a self-driving car crashes?' *The Irish Times*, 30 May 2019.

self-driven vehicle is involved in an accident that injures or kills someone. David Edmonds of the BBC told the *New Scientist* that he is convinced that, since technology in the area of automation is moving so quickly, we now need 'to work out quickly what ethics should be encoded into autonomous devices, and how machine ethics should be regulated'.[7]

In 2017, Arizona State passed a law requiring that the driver of an autonomous vehicle should be able to take control of the wheel if something goes wrong. This means that the driver is liable for prosecution if the car crashes into someone and injures or kills them. In spring 2018, the Ethics Commission of the Federal Ministry of Transport and Digital Infrastructure in the US released guidelines for self-driven cars. The commission included fourteen scientists and legal experts. One of the commission report's recommendations was that human life should always have priority over property or animal life. Another recommendation was that a surveillance system should record the activities of the self-driven vehicle in order to determine the cause of an accident. This would play the same role in the self-driven car that the so-called black box plays in an aircraft. If an accident takes place, then the police will examine the vehicle's surveillance system to establish what really happened.

Already, Germany has created ethical rules for autonomous vehicles that could provide a model for other countries.[8] In 2017, Alexander Dobrindt, the federal transport minister, presented a report on automated driving to the German cabinet. The report came from the Ethics Commission on Automated Driving, which was composed of ethicists, scientists and legal experts. It drew attention to the technological advances in autonomous vehicles that make them safer, thus reducing accidents and road injuries.

7 David Edmonds, 'Driverless cars still need a moral compass. But what kind?' *The Guardian*, 15 November 2018.

8 Peter Van Der Schaft, 'Germany Creates Ethics Rules for Autonomous Vehicles', *Robotics Business Review*, 30 May 2018 (https://www.roboticsbusinessreview.com/unmanned/germany-creates-ethics-rules-autonomous-vehicles).

It acknowledges that accidents will still happen, but states that human safety must take precedence over animals and property. The software in the autonomous vehicle must do everything possible to avoid accidents, but, if that is impossible, it should take a course of action that will do the least damage to humans. There must be no discrimination based on age, gender or race. The report is aware that some decisions are beyond the capability of the software. This is why it stipulates that a driver must be sitting behind the wheel to take control of the vehicle if difficulties arise. These measures or similar legislation will need to be introduced in most countries during the next few years to deal with the phenomenon of autonomous vehicles.

Testing Autonomous Vehicles

In June 2018, a £100,000 Ford Mondeo autonomous car, with a camera and multiple sensors, drove through the streets of Oxford in the UK. DRIVEN, the consortium developing autonomous transport in Britain, wanted to test this car on the narrow streets of Oxford, which are jam-packed with buses, cyclists and pedestrians. Sam Wong and Paul Newman are researchers at the University of Oxford where the self-driven Ford Mondeo had been developed. During the testing process a safety driver sat behind the wheel to take over if anything went wrong. On the roads outside Oxford, the car's Oxbotica control system, Selenium, proved excellent as the Ford Mondeo negotiated traffic lights, roundabouts and zebra crossings. During the journey, the only malfunction occurred when the car braked suddenly for no apparent reason. After the test, a researcher found that the car had braked because one of the sensors was confused by the light of the sun, as happened with the Tesla car in Florida. That sensor will not be used again.

Uber, BMW, Intel and many other automobile companies are investing significant amounts of money in developing self-driven cars and trucks. Håken Samuelsson, director of Volvo, predicts that by 2035 the use of autonomous cars will lead to an 80 per cent reduction in accidents. That company is currently testing autonomous cars in underground mines in northern Sweden, in partnership with the Swedish mining company, Boliden.[9]

A Word of Caution

Not everyone agrees that the widespread use of autonomous vehicles is imminent. Ola Benderim, an academic from the University of Gothenburg in Sweden, cautions that it will take more time and research to replace humans behind the wheel of trucks and cars.[10] Michiel van Ratigen, the secretary for the European New Car Assessment Programme Trials (Euro NCAP), agrees, and believes that autonomous vehicles, even with advanced driver assistance systems, need a vigilant, attentive driver behind the wheel at all times.[11] General Motors, which has invested millions of dollars in self-driven vehicles, has decided to postpone the introduction of their Cruise autonomous taxi, because of fears about its safety at the moment. It is clear that more research and tests are needed.

Despite the caution, almost all vehicle manufacturers around the world believe that, within fifteen years, the technologies described above will be fitted on all vehicles whether autonomous or driven by humans.

Electric Cars

Drivers who wish to abandon petrol or diesel vehicles have two fears. One is that their electric batteries will run out before they finish their journey, and the other is that charging the battery will take too long. Both of these challenges might be solved in the near future. Scientists at the Science Foundation, Ireland, Centre for Advanced Materials and BioEngineering Research (AMBER), have found an inexpensive way to make batteries more compact and quicker to

9 Kyran Fitzgerald, 'Time to wake up to the rise of the robot and its implications', *Irish Examiner*, 30 May 2016.

10 Ibid.

11 Neil Briscoe, op. cit.

charge. They have created batteries that have 250 per cent more energy density than any battery available today. Prior to this new breakthrough, battery manufacturers had already increased battery storage capacity by 3–5 per cent each year. This new research, which has gone far beyond that figure, is being led by Valeria Nicolosi, Professor of Nanomaterials and Advanced Microscopy at Trinity College, Dublin, and Jonathan Coleman, Professor of Chemical Physics at the same university. Their research will, hopefully, lead to new capacity for batteries to store more energy. It is presumed that a lot of the energy used to charge the batteries will come from renewable sources, such as sun, wind and wave. Nicolosi believes that 'the new, highly rechargeable battery is a game-changer in science'.[12] These new batteries, with larger storage capacity, will mean that we do not have to replace the batteries as often as heretofore, which will also benefit the environment.

In a world where climate change is increasing global temperatures, electric vehicles, both self-driven or human-driven models, will help lower the temperature in cities all over the world. Electric cars emit almost 21 per cent less heat than conventional cars.[13] In Beijing, in the summer of 2012, a team led by Canbing Li from Michigan State University, tested the hypothesis that conventional cars emit more heat than electric ones. They found that replacing conventional cars with electric ones in a city like Beijing would reduce global temperatures by one degree Celsius.

The Use of Cobalt in Electric Cars

Developing electric vehicles is not just about developing new technologies. There are also serious human rights problems that get little attention in the media. The batteries used to drive electric cars contain lithium and cobalt. Research by KU Leuven in Belgium and the University of Lubumbashi in the Democratic Republic

12 Peter McGuire, 'Battery breakthrough could help save the planet', *The Irish Times*, 20 June 2019.

13 'Electric cars may help keep cities cool', *New Scientist*, 28 March 2015.

of the Congo (DRC) found a high concentration of cobalt in the urine of people who lived near the cobalt mines. The researchers conducted a case study in Kasulo, an urban neighbourhood in Kolwezi, which is at the centre of the Congolese mining area. When one family discovered that there was cobalt containing ore under their house, the entire area quickly became a cobalt mine, resulting in dire medical consequences for the community. The main problem is that dust, which contains cobalt and other toxic metals, including uranium, is released during the mining process and settles on the ground. Cobalt dust causes asthma, decreased pulmonary function and fibrosis. According to Professor Memery, a medical toxicologist at the KU Leuven Department of Public Health and Primary Care, 'children living in the mining district have ten times as much cobalt in their urine than children living elsewhere'.[14]

It is also possible that in the DRC child labour is being used in the cobalt mining industry. According to the US Geological Survey, 50 per cent of the world's cobalt comes from that area. Amnesty International's research shows that there is a significant risk that cobalt mined by children ends up in the batteries of electric cars.

Cobalt is mostly mined as a by-product of copper or nickel. Why is cobalt important for batteries? Cobalt carries electric charges to and from the lithium, which is the other substance that is essential in batteries. Without cobalt, 'a battery is just a useless lump of metal and plastic'.[15] Mark Dummett, the business and human rights researcher of Amnesty International, has accused car makers of using cobalt from illegal mines in building their electric batteries. There is now a global search to find cobalt in other places in the world, apart from DRC. The results have been positive in both Idaho, in the US, and in Ontario, Canada. However, as battery production increases the demand for electric cars and trucks, it seems that there will be shortages of cobalt, especially if supplies from DRC are banned.

14 'Scientists reveal the hidden costs of cobalt mining in DR Congo', *EurekAlert*, 20 September 2018 (https://www.eurekalert.org/pub_releases/2018-09/kl-srt092018.php).

15 Neil Briscoe, 'Electric cars are not so "clean" after all', *The Irish Times*, 21 March 2018.

Self-driven Trucks

In Ireland, according to figures from the CSO, 147.2 million tonnes of goods were transported around the country by road in 2017.[16] In the same year, there were over six million trucks on the EU's roads.[17] The American Trucking Association estimates that there are approximately 3.5 million professional truck drivers in the US. The total number of people employed in the industry exceeds 8.5 million. The American Truckers' Association (ATA) believes it will need 90,000 more trucks annually for the next decade to keep up with demand.[18]

Globally, this is a huge industry, so the development of self-driven trucks will have a significant impact, not just on the trucking industry, but on the wider economy and society. In October 2018, an Uber trucking subsidiary named Otto delivered 2,000 cases of Budweiser beer from Fort Collins, Colorado, to Colorado Springs, a journey of 120 miles, without a driver at the wheel. Within a few years, this technology will go from prototype development to full production, and that means millions of truck drivers could be made redundant in the next fifteen to twenty years.

The impact of self-driven trucks will be felt in both the economy and society at large. Over the past number of decades, entire industries have been built around servicing trucks. These include motels, restaurants and filling stations. Truck driving is a job that does not require a college education and also pays a fairly good salary. In 2017, a truck driver in the US earned more than $40,000 per year.

Before the Covid-19 pandemic in 2020, the trucking industry was buoyant, and expected to grow in the short term. However, beyond that, the truck driving industry may be facing decline and,

16 *Road Freight Transport Survey 2017*, CSO (https://www.cso.ie/en/releasesandpublications/ep/p-rft/roadfreighttransportsurvey2017/).

17 Report *Vehicles in use – Europe 2017* (https://www.acea.be/statistics/article/vehicles-in-use-europe-2017).

18 The Schneider Guy, 'How Many Truck Drivers Are in the USA?' Schneider, 27 July 2018 (https://schneiderjobs.com/blog/driver/truck-drivers-in-usa).

possibly, extinction, because self-driven trucks are about to become more commonplace. The first self-driven truck arrived on US roads in the state of Nevada on 6 May 2015. Manufacturers of self-driven trucks emphasise that the safety of their trucks is their dominant concern. However, they also point out that self-driven trucks do not injure or kill as many people as regular trucks with human drivers. Self-driven trucks do not get tired, they do not consult their phones, drink alcohol or take drugs. In 2012, in the US, 330,000 large trucks were involved in accidents that killed 4,000 people. Around 90 per cent of these accidents were caused by driver error.[19]

US financial services group Morgan Stanley estimates that trucks will have complete autonomous capability by 2022, and massive penetration of the market will be achieved by 2026. Perhaps that time frame is too short, and the shift to autonomous trucks might not take place as quickly as Morgan Stanley estimates, but it is likely to come within a period of fifteen to twenty years. Trucking companies will want to reduce their costs by choosing self-driven trucks. If accidents are reduced, insurance premiums will fall, giving the owners of autonomous trucks a comparative advantage in the marketplace.

Conclusion

Taking all of these developments together, it appears that there will be a massive upheaval in this relatively well-paid industry within the next fifteen to twenty years.

19 Scott Santens, 'Self-Driving Trucks Are Going to Hit Us Like a Human-Driven Truck', *Medium*, 14 May 2015 (https://medium.com/basic-income/self-driving-trucks-are-going-to-hit-us-like-a-human-driven-truck-b8507d9c5961#.k04scv1eg).

Chapter 9
Robots and Warfare

Changing the Face of War

In 2014, at the start of the celebration of the centenary of the First World War, 888,246 ceramic poppies were placed around the Tower of London. That figure represented the number of British soldiers who were killed in the war. Some commentators made the point that the industrial nature of this slaughter, which took the lives of almost ten million soldiers worldwide, was due to a clash between nineteenth-century military tactics and the deadlier twentieth-century weapons. The manner in which the combatants lined up across from each other in the trenches was not particularly strategic, given the new military hardware that the armies had acquired during the previous decades.[1]

The first recoil-operated machine gun was invented by American-born British inventor Hiram Maxim in 1884. The British High Command saw no real use for the machine gun in warfare. On the other hand, the German military understood its potential, and had 12,000 machine guns available for its troops by the time the war began in August 1914. The extraordinarily lethal power of machine guns was demonstrated on the first day of the Battle of the Somme in 1916, when the British suffered a record 60,000 casualties, many of whom were mown down by machine-gun fire. It was the bloodiest day in the history of the British army. Few could have predicted the horrifying consequences of modern weaponry – tanks, machine guns and aircraft – all being used in tandem with out-of-date military tactics.

1 Editorial, 'A red line on robot war', *New Scientist*, 15 November 2014.

New Ways of Making War

Something similar is happening today. Many believe that future wars will not be fought like the Second World War, nor like the Iran–Iraq conflict in the 1980s where the individual armies fought each other. In these wars, the casualties were enormous, with Iran losing a million soldiers, and Iraq losing 300,000. This type of war will not happen again, because in the past two decades there has been a revolution in the development of new weaponry and delivery systems.

One of the major advances in weaponry has been the development of autonomous weapons. Today, killer robots can target and kill people thousands of miles away, without any human oversight. While all wars are destabilising for society, this kind of war is particularly so. Automatic weapons are being developed and deployed by a number of countries, including China, Israel, South Korea, Russia, the UK and the US.

The Use of Drones for Surveillance and Combat

Shortly after 9/11, the US began sending drones into foreign airspace to kill suspected terrorists. At first, the strikes were confined to Afghanistan, but later this was extended to Pakistan, Yemen and Somalia. These decisions were supported by Presidents Obama and Trump, even though many commentators argued that they were illegal.[2] The proliferation of drones and other similar technologies means that military power is no longer exclusive to rich countries. It is now available to all countries and to terrorists, criminals and insurgents. All of these now use drones and other cost-effective technologies to wreak havoc on their targets. In 2018, Islamic State (IS) successfully used drones to conduct surveillance in Syria and to carry grenades in the battle for Mosul city. Many countries use robots to provide the army with surveillance and to disarm bombs. In some situations, robots can enter a building

2 Editorial, 'Drone warfare strikes back', *New Scientist*, 1 July 2017.

ahead of human soldiers and disarm any bombs left there by terrorists or others.[3]

The US and Drone Warfare

The US has used drones to conduct extra-territorial lethal operations during the past fifteen years. Robert George, of Princeton University, has spoken several times about the use of drones. In June 2012, George critiqued the Obama administration's use of drones in civilian areas. According to George, while the use of drones is not inherently immoral in otherwise justifiable military operations, the risk of death and other grave harm to non-combatants complicates the situation.[4] He believes that having a valid military target is not a sufficient justification for the use of weapons such as killer drones. He is clear that the wholesale and indiscriminate use of drones cannot be justified and should be critiqued, challenged and abandoned.[5]

Probably the most dangerous drone assignation took place in early January 2020, when, with the permission of President Trump, Major General Qassim Suleimani, Iran's top military and intelligence commander, was assassinated in a drone attack at Baghdad International Airport. While most Republican politicians supported President Trump's action, Democrat Senator Christopher S. Murphy of Connecticut criticised the President's decision to assassinate the second most powerful person in Iran, knowing that this might set off a major regional war that could have serious consequences for millions of people.[6]

3 Chris Baraniuk, 'World War R', *New Scientist*, 15 November 2014.
4 'Catholics see moral complications in drone usage', Catholic News Agency (CAN), 12 March 2013 (https://www.catholicnewsagency.com/news/catholics-see-moral-complications-in-drone-usage).
5 Ibid.
6 Michael Crowley, Falih Hassan and Eric Schmitt, 'Strike in Iraq Kills Qassim Suleimani, Commander of Iranian Forces', *The New York Times*, 2 January 2020. (https://www.nytimes.com/2020/01/02/world/middleeast/qassem-soleimani-iraq-iran-attack.html).

The US Navy and Killer Weapons

The US navy has developed the Phalanx anti-missile system aboard its Aegis ships. This system can perform its own 'kill assessment' without the involvement of military personnel. Christof Heyns, of South Africa, who is the UN's Special Rapporteur for extrajudicial executions, feels that allowing robots to kill, without any human authorisation, would contravene humanitarian law. In fact, according to him, 'humans need to be quite closely involved in the decision for it not to violate human rights'.[7]

Some military analysts believe that autonomous drones are the most significant development in military technology since the creation of atomic and nuclear weapons in the 1940s and early 1950s. Regrettably, swarms of autonomous drones, run by AI, are now being developed by many armies. Some commentators see this move as one of the most serious problems facing humankind, and, unfortunately, there is not enough serious discussion about it.

The Development of Killer Drones in Other Countries

In the UK, the Royal Air Force (RAF) is in the process of developing its own crewless jets, called Taranis. These jets can fly to a particular place and observe objects of interest, with little intervention from ground operators. The Russian army has its own 'mobile robotic complex'. This is a crewless tank-like vehicle which guards ballistic missile installations against attack. Dodaam Systems, a South Korean arms manufacturer, has developed what is called the Super Aegis II gun turret. This piece of armoury can detect and fire on moving targets without any human intervention. It can pinpoint someone's location at a distance of 2.2 kilometres and fire on them.[8]

At present, more than thirty nation-states possess, or are developing, armed drones for military use. In this new AI-led arms

7 Ibid.

8 Jamie Smyth and Bryan Harris, 'Academics warn of killer robot's arms race', *Financial Times*, 5 April 2018 (International) (https://www.ft.com/content/6ef206e6-37d1-11e8-8b98-2f31af407cc8).

race, many governments are fearful that they might fall behind other nations in not having these new technologies, but they are also nervous about the ethical issues involved.[9] Politicians fear that, as people become more aware of the potential for drone and robot warfare, many might take to the streets to demand that these weapons be banned immediately. In recent times, there have been persistent calls by civil society, religious groups and the European Parliament for the EU to adopt a common policy on the use of armed drones. In June 2017, the European Defence Fund announced a new multibillion euro fund to foster cooperation among member states, as they acquire and develop unmanned systems, drone technology and related satellite communications. The possibility of EU states developing this technology, without a shared understanding of its lawful use, worries civil society and religious groups because of its potential to violate international law, to create chaos and anarchy and kill thousands of people.[10] In October 2018, a statement was presented to the UN on behalf of fifty-four civil society organisations and twenty countries, criticising these new weapons because they violate international human rights and humanitarian law.[11]

The Depersonalisation of Mass Killing

Professor Christof Heyns, from the University of Pretoria in South Africa, argues that if these very destructive new weapons are not ultimately controlled by humans, it could result in the 'depersonalisation of force'. In a 2013 report to the UN, he warned that these 'tireless war machines, ready for deployment at the push of a button' could lead to a future of permanent global conflict. If governments do not have to put boots on the ground, sending

9 Peter Apps, 'Amid ethical fears, China and Russia ahead in AI arms race,' *The Irish Examiner*, 16 January 2019 (https://www.irishexaminer.com/breakingnews/views/analysis/amid-ethical-fears-china-and-russia-ahead-in-ai-arms-race-897836.html).

10 Jack McDonald, 'Drones and the European Union Prospects for a Common Future', Chatham House, The Royal Institute of International Affairs, February 2018.

11 Joint civil society statement on drones UN General Assembly First Committee on Disarmament and International Security, 17 October 2018 (https://s3.amazonaws.com/unoda-web/wp-content/uploads/2018/10/17Oct-drones.pdf).

in soldiers who might be wounded or killed, going to war could become too easy.[12]

More than fifty of the world's leading robotic experts are boycotting the South Korean Advanced Institute of Science and Technology (KAIST) and its defence manufacturer, Hanwha Systems, over their decision to open an AI weapons laboratory that will accelerate the arms race by developing more powerful autonomous weapons.[13]

Opposition to Lethal Autonomous Weapons

The global campaign to Stop Killer Robots began in April 2013. It urged governments and the UN to outlaw the development of lethal autonomous weapons systems. The initiative is also referred to as LAWS. Several countries with sophisticated military weapons, such as South Korea, the US, Britain and Russia oppose the ban, because they believe that existing international and humanitarian law is sufficient in this area. Governments were invited to attend a Convention on Conventional Weapons (CCW) in Geneva in November 2018 to discuss the use of lethal autonomous weapons systems, and how they might ultimately be banned. The Secretary General of the UN, António Guterres, called for a ban on killer robots, stating that 'for me there is a message that is very clear: these machines which have the power to take human lives are politically unacceptable, morally repugnant, and should be banned by international law'.[14]

In November 2017, Stuart Russell, a leading AI scientist at the University of California in Berkeley, screened a film at the UN Convention on Conventional Weapons, hosted by the Campaign to Stop Killer Robots. Russell is convinced that the manufacture and use of autonomous weapons such as drones, tanks and automated

12 Jamie Smyth and Bryan Harris, 'Academics warn of killer robot arms race', *Financial Times*, 4 April 2018.
13 Jane Wakefield, 'South Korean university boycotted over "killer robots"', BBC, 5 April 2018 (https://www.bbc.com/news/technology-43653648).
14 Remarks at 'Web Summit', UN Secretary-General, 8 November 2018.

machine guns would undermine human security and freedom. He warned people that the window of opportunity to stop this development of autonomous weapons is closing very fast.[15]

In July 2018, over 200 technology companies and 3,000 individuals signed a public pledge not to participate in or support the development, manufacture, trade or use of lethal autonomous weapons.[16] In 2018, Kate Conger, who worked as a journalist covering cybersecurity and privacy for Gizmodo and TechCrunch before moving to *The New York Times*, reported that Google was involved in Project Maven, which was making autonomous weapons for the US Department of Defence. As a result, several Google employees resigned and 4,000 other employees sent a letter to Google's chief executive, Sundar Pichal, demanding that the company withdraw immediately from warfare technology.[17] As a result, Google developed a set of ethical principles for AI, which included a commitment not to develop AI for use in weapons.

However, Aaron Rogan, a journalist with the *Sunday Business Post* in Ireland, reveals that Google still works on US military projects.[18] Laura Nolan, an Irish software engineer who resigned from Google over the Pentagon's Project Maven, told the *Post* that she was asked by her managers to develop computer systems that could be used in autonomous weapons. If this were done, Google, would then expect more contracts from the US military. Nolan said, 'A lot of us were being asked to work on changes that could eventually support the processing of military data on Google Cloud. That made us think that they wanted to do more nefarious things and keep them

15 Ian Sample, 'Ban on killer robots urgently needed, say scientists', *The Guardian*, 13 November 2017 (https://www.theguardian.com/science/2017/nov/13/ban-on-killer-robots-urgently-needed-say-scientists).

16 Gibbs Samuel, 'Musk, Wozniak and Hawking urge ban on warfare AI and autonomous weapons', *The Guardian*, 27 July 2015.

17 Scott Shane and Daisuke Wakabayashi, 'The Business of War: Google Employees Protest Work for the Pentagon', *The New York Times*, 4 April 2018.

18 Aaron Rogan, 'Google's Dublin workers asked to work on US drone warfare project', *Sunday Business Post*, 5–6 May 2019.

under wraps.'[19] Nolan is critical of Google. She told Marie Boran, a journalist with *The Irish Times*, that Google 'made big noises about organising the world's information to make it useful and accessible – not for killing people'.[20] Nolan dismisses the ethics boards of many technology companies, because 'they are designed in a non-transparent way that gives the appearance of adherence to ethical guidelines, while not having to comply with anything or be accountable to an external committee. They seem to want to have their cake and eat it.'[21]

Banning Autonomous Lethal Weapons

Given the potential dangers to local and global security, the first step towards banning autonomous weapons would be to lobby politicians worldwide. In the 1960s, scientists convinced both President Lyndon Johnson and President Richard Nixon to renounce the US biological weapons programme, which led to the setting up of the Biological Weapons Convention (BWC). This was the first multilateral disarmament treaty to ban the development, production and stockpiling of weapons of mass destruction. The treaty opened for signature on 10 April 1972 and came into force on 26 March 1975.

Noel Sharkey, Emeritus Professor of AI at Sheffield University, has been warning the public about the power of autonomous weapons since 2007. He stated that the film associated with the campaign to Stop Killer Robots 'made my hair stand on end as it crystallises one possible futuristic outcome from the development of these hi-tech weapons. There is an emerging arms race among the hi-tech nations to develop autonomous submarines, fighter jets, battleships and tanks that can find their own targets and apply violent force without the involvement of meaningful human decisions. It will

19 Ibid.
20 Marie Boran, 'Autonomous weapons are not science fiction – they're here', *The Irish Times*, 11 July 2019.
21 Ibid.

only take one major war to unleash these new weapons with tragic humanitarian consequences and destabilisation of global security.'[22]

At a meeting in Geneva, Switzerland, in December 2015, Archbishop Silvano Tomasi, the Permanent Observer of the Holy See at the UN in Geneva, warned that respect for and compliance with international humanitarian law is increasingly being ignored in many countries. 'The principles of the law have at best become a mesmerising litany,' he said. 'Great principles are not able to ensure justice and peace. When they prove to be ineffective, we simply criticise their application.'[23] The most urgent issue on the agenda for discussion at the event was the proposed ban on fully autonomous weapons.[24] By 2018, twenty-two countries had called for an outright ban on automatic weapons because they believe that if this does not happen there will be an escalation in their use and development, which would make the world a much more insecure place for everyone.

Drones Are Cheap

As military budgets are diminishing, military personnel and politicians realise that the cost of maintaining soldiers has risen considerably. For example, each soldier assigned to Afghanistan in 2012 cost $2.1 million to maintain. That figure is quite high, even when medical and other related costs are factored in. Because of advances in medicine, soldiers now have a much better chance of surviving war, even when they incur serious battleground injuries. In the Iraq and Afghan wars, for every seven soldiers injured, just one died because better medical facilities were available to them. The greater survival rate of soldiers today means that there is a need

22 Ian Sample, 'Ban on killer robots urgently needed, say Scientists', *The Guardian*, 13 November 2017 (https://www.theguardian.com/science/2017/nov/13/ban-on-killer-robots-urgently-needed-say-scientists).

23 'Killer robots? They're a real issue – and here's what the Vatican has to say', Catholic News Agency, December 2015 (https://www.catholicnewsagency.com/news/killer-robots-theyre-a-real-issue-and-heres-what-the-vatican-has-to-say-75653).

24 Ibid.

for long-term medical care. Because most soldiers who are injured are in their twenties, the cost of their rehabilitation can continue for thirty, forty or even fifty years. With medical costs rising every year, one can see why military planners are looking seriously at a soldier-less mode of military operations in the future. Therefore, the move to use robots, drones and other automatic weapons in warfare is driven by economic as well as operational motives.

Conclusion

In this chapter, I have argued that if drones and robots become a central part of our military strategies, there will be no need to have huge national armies, because drones will carry out surveillance and make the decisions to attack and kill people. The use of killer drones is immoral, and we need a global ban on their production and deployment before enormous and, possibly, irreversible damage is done to humanity and to our planet.

Unfortunately, there is still not enough public awareness, even in the media, of the potential risks of lethal autonomous weapons, and the concerns that these weapons could be used by terrorists and criminal gangs in every part of the world. If drones and autonomous weapons are adopted by terrorist groups, it will be almost impossible to control their use. The best option is to ban them now, and religious and civic leaders should play a central role in bringing this situation about.

Chapter 10
Universal Basic Income (UBI)

In December 2016, Seán Ward from Social Justice Ireland delivered a paper on Universal Basic Income (UBI) at the Social Justice Ireland's Conference. He defined UBI as 'a substantial, unconditional and tax-free payment from the exchequer to all citizens on an individual basis, financed by a flat tax on all income. It would replace tax credits and tax allowances for those in paid employment and welfare payments for those who are not in paid employment.'[1]

In 2018, the Institute for Fiscal Studies (IFS)in Britain stated that 'above-inflation increases in Britain's minimum wage are putting a rising number of workers at risk of being replaced by machines'.[2] Financial journalist Larry Elliott suggests one of the best ways of tackling this issue of people not being able to find paid employment is by giving a UBI, because the rise of automation means that there will be less work for people.[3]

Development economist Guy Standing is a leading advocate for UBI, and a co-founder of the Basic Income Earth Network. From 1975 to 2006, he worked at the International Labour Organisation in Geneva, where he witnessed the devastating impact of globalisation on the poor of the world and the shrinking prospects for the world's middle classes. He believes that there has been an upsurge of interest in UBI in the last few years for several reasons.[4] Firstly, many people are alarmed by the spread of populism, with the election of Donald Trump as president of the US in 2016, the election of

1 Sean Ward, 'History and Recent Developments on Basic Income in Ireland', in *Radical Utopia or Practical Solution?*, Dublin: Social Justice Ireland, 2016, 77.
2 Larry Elliott, 'More jobs at risk of automation if minimum wage rises, IFS warns', *The Guardian*, 4 January 2018.
3 Ibid.
4 John Thornhill, 'Elite fears over tech universal debate', *Financial Times*, 3 May 2017.

Rodrigo Duterte in the Philippines in 2016 and the election of Jair Bolsonaro in Brazil in 2017. The 2018 parliamentary elections in Hungary were a victory for the right-wing populist party, Fidesz-KDNP, with Viktor Orbán remaining as prime minister. Narendra Modi is a Hindu Nationalist and a member of the Bharatiya Janata Party (BJP). He was re-elected as prime minister in India in 2019, with an even larger mandate than the party received in the 2014 elections. His party won 353 seats, as against ninety-one for the Indian National Congress.

It is clear that these leaders will not address the fundamental problems in society today, namely inequality, mass unemployment and enormous environmental degradation.

Furthermore, new technologies are undermining many of our current jobs, even though during 2019, there was close to full employment in the UK, the US and Ireland.[5] That changed dramatically with the arrival of Covid-19 in 2020.[6]

With the development of robots, drones and machine-learning, blue-collar jobs are not the only ones that will gradually disappear. Increasing automation will begin to encroach on other sectors as well. In the future, many people will not have a job, or will have only a part-time job that will not support their basic needs. A better education with degrees from a third-level institution will not guarantee a well-paid permanent job. In 2015, more than 20 per cent of graduates in the US were overqualified for their current jobs because more and more jobs are at risk through automation. As a result of this trend, the income for most graduates has also fallen during the past decade.[7]

The same reality obtains in many European countries, where university education is often free, unlike in the US.[8] There is a need for a global conversation on how the fruits of labour will be

5 Ibid.
6 Ibid.
7 Larry Elliott, op. cit.
8 Martin Ford, *The Rise of the Robots – Technology and the Threat of Mass Unemployment*, London: Oneworld Publications, 2015, 249.

distributed in a fair and equitable way.[9] Martin Ford, author of *The Rise of the Robots – Technology and the Threat of Mass Unemployment*, is convinced that 'the skills ladder is not really a ladder at all; it is a pyramid, and there is only so much room at the top'.[10]

UBI: The Argument in Favour

Traditionally, the case for UBI was made on the grounds of equity, to bridge the gap between rich and poor. It was supported by socialists, feminists and left-leaning academics and was seen to recognise the value of caring for children and elderly relatives. Supporters of UBI claim that it will eliminate the poverty trap while, at the same time, making sure that no one is financially better off unemployed, because income from work should always be greater than that provided by UBI.

Those who support UBI point out that it will give more bargaining power to the individual workers in dealing with their employers than would have been conferred by membership of a trade union. It also means that workers do not have to accept just any kind of job from an employer in order to earn a basic wage that will meet their needs in supporting a family, so it will create a more equal relationship between employers and employees. This, in turn, will lead to better working conditions – the constant demand for flexibility in the modern workplace does not always favour the employee.

Economists Joel Mokyr, Chris Vickers and Nicolas L. Ziebarth have written on the impact of technological changes in the modern economy. They note that increased employment flexibility can be a mixed blessing. On the one hand, it can help in balancing the demands of work and family. Alternatively, it can be a back door for employers to extract more effort from employees with the expectation that they are always accessible on their mobile phones.[11] A 2017 editorial in *The New York Times* stated that 'in reality there is

9 Hal Hodson, 'All Plan and No Work', *New Scientist*, 25 June 2016.
10 Ford, op. cit., 250.
11 Tim Dunlop, *Why the Future is Workless*, Kensington, NSW: New South, 2016, 166–67.

no utopia at companies like Uber, Lyft, Instacart and Hady, whose workers are often manipulated into working long hours for low wages while continually chasing the next ride or task'.[12]

The Pew Research Centre is a nonpartisan US think tank based in Washington, DC. It produces information on social issues, opinions and demographic trends that shape the US and the wider world. In 2017, it found that workers in the 'gig' economy tended to be poor and were more likely to be members of minority groups, rather than the population at large. Crucially, since workers for most 'gig' economy companies are considered independent contractors and not employees, they do not qualify for basic protections such as overtime pay and minimum wages.[13] This is why a company such as Uber, which commenced operations in 2009, could grow to 700,000 contractors by 2014. Reflecting on the impact of the 'gig' economy on workers, *The New York Times* editorial ends on an ominous note. It says that 'experience with these companies shows that without legal protections and ethical norms that once were widely accepted, workers will find the economy of the future an even more inhospitable place'.[14]

UBI recognises all kinds of work, not merely work for which people are paid an income. In almost every culture, work in the home, which in the past has been done mainly by women, involves cooking, cleaning and caring for children. It is invariably unpaid. Feminists have been promoting UBI since its introduction as it would mean that this crucial work would be valued by everyone in society.

Eamon Murphy and Sean Ward, in an article on the costing of a UBI for Ireland, argue that UBI is much more effective than other kinds of social assistance in supplementing the incomes of poor people.[15]

12 'The Gig Economy's False Promise', *The New York Times*, 10 April 2017 (https://www.nytimes.com/2017/04/10/opinion/the-gig-economys-false-promise.html).
13 Ibid.
14 Ibid.
15 Eamon Murphy and Seán Ward, 'Costing a Basic Income for Ireland', in *Radical Utopia or Practical Solution?* op. cit., 133.

Some people disagree with the idea of UBI because they assert that it will cause major migration of people to countries that have introduced it, overwhelming their resources. Sister Brigid Reynolds and Dr Seán Healy counter this argument by pointing out that 'the conditions that would apply to new migrants receiving these payments – these are the same conditions as currently apply to migrants becoming eligible for social welfare payments once they arrive in a country. Such conditions apply both within the EU and beyond its borders.'[16]

The Long History of UBI

Thomas Paine (1737–1809) was an English-born political theorist and revolutionary whose influential pamphlet helped inspire the American Revolution. In his 1797 pamphlet *Agrarian Justice* he envisioned the creation of a national fund through levying a ground rent on landowners in the US. Paine proposed that those who owned cultivated land owed the community a ground rent. From this tax, two kinds of payments would be made to each person. Everyone would receive £15 when they reached the age of twenty-one as a way of supporting them at the threshold of adulthood. Later in life, at the age of fifty, they would receive an annual sum of £10 to help them in their old age.

Another advantage of UBI is that the administration costs would be quite low compared with the bureaucracy and cost of administering our current welfare system. Each developed economy has a complex welfare system, which is often difficult to understand and costly to implement. For example, a Freedom of Information request in 2012 revealed that the Department of Work and Pensions in Britain spent £5.3 billion on administration. This amounts to 3.5 per cent of its total budget.[17] This money could be used to fund UBI.

Austrian-born Friedrich August von Hayek (1899–1992) studied

16 Ibid., 24.
17 Tim Dunlop, op. cit., 153.

law and economics in Vienna. He believed that the wealth of society came from entrepreneurship and innovation and that these were possible only in a society that promoted free markets. In 1932, he became the Tooke Professor of Economic Science and Statistics at the London School of Economics and remained there until 1950. He spent a number of years at Cambridge University, an during his time there, he and John Kenneth Galbraith disagreed on many aspects of economic policy. Later, von Hayek taught in the University of Chicago. In 1974, he shared the Nobel Prize for economic science with Gunnar Myrdal. He opposed socialism and the welfare state because he believed that they would inevitably lead to totalitarianism. However, he supported the idea of UBI, mainly because he believed that it would protect individual liberty. For Hayek, UBI would allow people an opportunity to relate to the market on their own terms, rather than being dependent on welfare meted out by governments.

In 2015, the US libertarian think tank, Cato Institute, issued a report supporting, in principle, the idea of a national income. They argued that the complex welfare system, which costs almost $1 trillion each year, has failed. Anti-poverty programmes administered by 126 federal, state and local governments have been unsuccessful.[18]

Milton Friedman joined the faculty of economics at the University of Chicago in 1946. He and other members of the faculty were staunch advocates of laissez-faire economics, which states that economics and business function best when there is no interference from governments, and when governments espouse free trade. In the next few decades, what became known as the Chicago School blossomed into one of the most influential schools of economics across the world. Still Milton Friedman supported UBI. He believed that it would reduce the coercive power of the state, promote individual freedom and remove wasteful government bureaucracy, especially around welfare payments.

18 Thornhill, op. cit.

Covid-19 and the Jettisoning of Neo-liberal Economics

In March 2020, in the early days of the Covid-19 pandemic in Europe, many governments abandoned neo-liberal economics and borrowed enormous sums of money to protect their citizens, workers and the wider economy. This did not happen because a socialist revolution had spread across the world. There were no demonstrations or riots on the streets. This extraordinary reversal was brought about by conservative politicians and conservative institutions, such as the World Bank and the IMF. In a period of just two weeks during March 2020, Rishi Sunak, Chancellor of the Exchequer in Britain, borrowed £60 billion to minimise the impact of Covid-19 on the UK economy and its citizens.[19]

Similarly, on 27 March 2020, the US House of Representatives passed legislation enabling a historic $2.2 trillion stimulus package to help business survive the pandemic. The package included a cheque of $1,200 for almost everyone in the US, and an extra $600 a week for those who were not working. $650 billion was made available to support businesses, states and cities across the country.[20]

By the end of March 2020, more than eighty countries had sought financial aid from the IMF. The head of the IMF, Kristalina Georgieva, said that the Covid-19 crisis was as serious as the global financial crash in 2008/09. In less than a month, Covid-19 had transformed the world economic system in a way that no one could have predicted in January 2020. David McWilliams, an Irish economist, and Joe Lynam from the BBC, characterised the enormity of the economic change in these actions. 'Just as the calendar was bifurcated into BC and AD, the economic future will delineate into two eras; ante-corona (AC) and post-corona (PC).'[21] I believe that in this new economic climate, it will be much easier to promote the benefits of UBI in a PC economic world.

19 Chris Gilles, 'Sundak tops up rescue fund to £650bn', *Financial Times*, 28 March 2020.
20 Lauren Fedor, 'US House approves $2tn stimulus', *Financial Times*, 28 March 2020.
21 David McWilliams and Joe Lynam, 'World will need a new financial system after this', *The Irish Times*, 25 March 2020.

Spain Creates a Universal Minimum Income

On 28 May 2020, in response to the Covid-19 pandemic, the Deputy Prime Minister of Spain, Pablo Iglesias, announced that the Spanish government had decided to support a national minimum income to cater for the needs of the nation's 850,000 lowest income households. Each family will receive €500 a month. The government estimates that the initiative will help support 2.3 million people and will cost about three billion euro a year. In announcing the plan, Iglesias said, 'Today is a historic day for our democracy. Today this government is showing that its political choice is social justice, and it takes the Constitution seriously.'[22]

Support for UBI in Silicon Valley

In recent years, tech entrepreneurs at Silicon Valley have shown an interest in UBI. Sam Altman, the US entrepreneur, investor and programmer, is the former president of Y Combinator. Y Combinator is a start-up company which was launched in 2005. In the past fifteen years, it has provided capital to launch over 2,000 start-up companies, many in the technology area, including Stripe, Airbnb, Cruise Automation and Dropbox. It might seem strange that a Silicon Valley company is backing UBI, but many of these entrepreneurs have talked about their dream of changing the world so that it can be a better place for everyone.[23]

However, we must be cautious about the suggestion that big tech firms are intent on bettering the world. As we saw in the introduction, many large companies are promoting surveillance capitalism. Big tech firms make a lot of money on their platforms by streaming news from other media companies without paying a fair price for it. This practice is decimating media companies all over the world.

22 Kristin Toussaint, 'Spain creates a universal minimum income targeted at 2.3 million people, FASTCOMPANY, 28 May 2020 (https://www.fastcompancom/90511093/spain-creates-a-universal-minimum-income-targeted-at-2-3-million-people).

23 Richard Waters, 'Silicon valley engineers a solution to wealth divide', *Financial Times*, 3 May 2017.

Bill Gates and UBI

Bill Gates believes that because robots are taking human jobs they should be taxed in the same way as workers are at the moment. It is through taxation that governments raise revenue to run the state and finance the employment of teachers, doctors, police and other public servants.

Gates is aware of the challenges posed by the McKinsey report, published in January 2017. This report found that 50 per cent of jobs performed by humans are vulnerable, and they will be replaced by robots within the next twenty years or so. This would amount to a loss of about $15 trillion in wages worldwide and about $2.7 trillion in the US alone. Losing this kind of money and the taxes associated with it would be catastrophic for any modern democracy. Gates is convinced that robots should be welcomed by humans because their introduction will give people more time to care for children or older people. This care will become more necessary in future decades as life expectancy rises. Once automation takes over activities that humans used to do, this should free up time to 'do a better job of reaching out to the elderly, having smaller class sizes in schools, helping children with special needs'.[24] These roles, Gates says, require human levels of empathy, and there is a current shortage of people who can fill them.

The publication of the Global Commission on Adaptation (GCA) on the impact of climate change in September 2019 makes it abundantly clear that the world remains unprepared for a changed climate.[25] Much work also needs to be done to stop the destruction of biodiversity and protect and rehabilitate ecologically run-down areas of the planet. Again, there would be plenty of work for everyone to do, but many people who do these jobs today do not get paid.[26]

In 2008, Kathryn Myronuk was one of the founder members of

24 Ibid.

25 Damian Carrington, 'World remains "gravely" unprepared for climate crisis', *The Guardian*, 10 September 2019.

26 Ibid.

the Singularity University (SU) at NASA Research Park in Silicon Valley. For years, she has encouraged corporate tech executives to address some of the basic challenges facing society, especially hunger, homelessness and environmental degradation. She also makes the point that many of these executives are interested in UBI because they are aware that their technologies will lead to greater automation and, therefore, fewer jobs for humans.[27]

These companies are probably aware that if automation continues apace, and people are not employed in traditional jobs, they simply will not have the money to buy goods and services. In such a scenario, only the super-rich, who constitute a small segment of society, would have the money to buy the goods and services on offer in the marketplace. Without UBI, vast numbers of people would have no purchasing power and would be locked into a dangerous poverty trap that would be very detrimental to democracy.

Arguments Against UBI

Those who are against UBI, such as the Conservative Party in Britain, see it as a disincentive to work because it seems to be rewarding idleness and, therefore, undermining the economy. The research to date does not support this thesis, and, I presume that whoever wrote this report would have been horrified at the thought of Tory chancellor Rishi Sunak giving at least £60 billion in extra public spending to fight Covid-19.

There is a danger, however, that if everyone gets UBI, many people might not be willing to make the effort to continue their studies up to third level. Martin Ford, in *The Rise of the Robots*, gives the example of an academically struggling secondary school student who knows that they will receive a guaranteed income, regardless of whether or not he or she continues their education. That, obviously, creates a powerful and perverse disincentive to achieving one's full potential. For this reason, Ford suggests we ought to pay a somewhat

27 Ibid.

higher income to those who pass A levels (or the equivalent).[28] Ford is certain that, if we reach the point where the links between education and securing a good job are not as clear as they were in the past, society may value education as a public good in itself, and tailor policies and creative programmes to promote it.

UBI in Brazil and India

Research into the income support system in Brazil, called Bolsa Família, found that most people spent their cash sensibly, especially when it was given to the women in families.[29] There were similar positive results from a UBI programme in India in 2013, which was funded by UNICEF and the World Bank. Two villages were chosen where adults were paid 200 rupees per month, later increased to 300 rupees. The children were paid 150 rupees. Professor Guy Standing, from the University of London, monitored the programme and wrote about it. He highlighted many positive results. At a basic level, many people used the money to improve their homes, and took precautions to avoid contracting malaria, by removing stagnant water lying near their houses. Households improved their diet by eating more fruit and vegetables, which they would not have been able to afford in the past. As a result, there was a major improvement in the health of children and, especially, girls. Better health, and a little more money, made it possible for children to attend school regularly. Adults often used this money to improve their own working conditions. Many men abandoned casual labour and began working in agriculture or in small retail businesses for themselves. Some women used the money to buy sewing machines and started a dressmaking business.

UBI empowers people because it gives them the opportunity to make choices that can improve their lives, which, in turn, builds up their confidence. This often does not happen with the current

28 Martin Ford, op. cit., 262.
29 Ibid., 157.

welfare programmes, because bureaucrats, who are not familiar with the daily pressures that poor people face, are often more concerned about following proper procedures and filling out the proper forms. One of the better outcomes of UBI is that the participants are able to avoid borrowing from moneylenders, who normally charge huge interest rates which ensure continued indebtedness.[30] This is a major change, as I know from working with credit unions in Mindanao, in the Philippines, during the 1980s. When people are in debt to moneylenders, they live from hand to mouth, and cannot improve their life situation.

In India, UBI payments helped people to make use of the money to better themselves and their families. The only obligation for those participating in the programme in India was that, within three months, they had to open a bank account, or an account in a cooperative, into which the money would be paid. Many of those managing the programme felt that this could not be achieved because those involved in the scheme had never had any reason to approach a bank or a credit institution in the past. To the total surprise of the advisory board, 98 per cent of those involved opened a bank account within three months, and the rest followed suit soon afterwards.[31]

UBI for Ireland

Anne Ryan is a lecturer at the Department of Adult and Community Education at NUI, Maynooth, and a member of a group called Basic Income Ireland. According to Ryan, UBI should be sufficient to support a frugal, but decent, lifestyle.[32] It would replace social welfare payments for people who are unemployed, and for people who are employed, the UBI payment would replace most tax credits.

30 Ibid., 158–60.

31 Guy Standing, 'Basic income paid to the poor can transform lives', *The Guardian*, 18 December 2014 (https://www.theguardian.com/business/economics-blog/2014/dec/18/incomes-scheme-transforms-lives-poor).

32 Anne Ryan, 'How we could abolish all welfare and introduce a basic income for everyone', *The Journal.ie*, 5 December 2015 (http://www.thejournal.ie/readme/abolish-social-welfare-basic-income-2483562-Dec2015/).

The payment would also extend to those who currently receive no income from the state.

UBI could give security to entrepreneurs who might wish to live in small towns or rural areas across Ireland, rather than follow the present trend of migrating to the cities, especially to Dublin. This would have the added benefit of allowing families to remain living and working on the family farm, especially when the income from the farm cannot support a family. UBI would also support artists and craftspeople living in rural or small urban communities. This simple change would have huge social, cultural and sporting benefits for rural Ireland. In recent years, migration from rural areas has meant that parishes can no longer field a hurling or football team. Furthermore, UBI would reduce the need to build massive housing estates in the cities. The experience of people who had to work from home during the Covid-19 crisis should also help to make this transition achievable.

Anne Ryan refers to a 2015 report by Social Justice Ireland, which calculated that, operating within the current social welfare rates in the Republic of Ireland, UBI could be paid as follows: each person between twenty-five and sixty-five would receive €188 per week. The amount would increase to €230 for those over sixty-five. Younger people between eighteen and twenty-five would receive €100 each week, and the child benefit rates would remain as they are at the moment. Carers' Allowances, Disability Allowance and other special needs payments would still exist as means-tested top-ups to UBI. Basic Income Ireland favours €200 per week, and it has suggested a flat 45 per cent tax to pay for the introduction of UBI in Ireland. While many would consider this to be a huge financial burden on taxpayers it would certainly be a massive boost to those on low incomes.[33]

In its campaign for the general election in 2016, Fianna Fáil promised to give everyone in Ireland €188 per week, irrespective

33 Fiona Reddan, 'Should everyone be paid €752 a month for doing nothing?' *The Irish Times*, 14 June 2016.

of their current income.[34] The pledge was to be incorporated into the party's election manifesto. The party insisted it would be a 'red line issue' for any other party or group who would wish to govern with them. Fianna Fáil promised to set up an expert group to report within six months on what the size of the proposed payment would be, and what kind of changes in taxation would be needed to fund the initiative. The basic minimum income would be presented as a major protection against poverty, especially since permanent and well-paying jobs were becoming difficult to find, and this situation would, most probably, continue. Any income that might be earned above what the party called this minimum welfare payment, would be taxed at a fixed rate, possibly around 25 per cent.

Willie O'Dea, the Fianna Fáil spokesperson on Social Protection and Social equality, pointed out that the then current welfare bill stood at about €30 billion per annum. Mr O'Dea claimed that UBI would replace 'virtually every non-pension welfare payment, except disability and housing benefits'.[35] He felt that UBI would make it possible to scrap the complex and contradictory welfare codes that currently exist. It would also cut down on the administrative bureaucracy involved in means-testing people who apply for benefits. This, in turn, would help eliminate fraud.

Fianna Fáil claims that many sections of the population already receive welfare payments. These include non-contributory pensions, child benefit and unemployment allowances. For this reason, Fianna Fáil believes that the total cost of the UBI might not exceed the amount already being spent on current welfare benefits. One of the favourable outcomes would be to 'remove the poverty trap disincentives built into the current system, where taking a job can leave you financially worse off'.[36] However, since 2016, Fianna Fáil

34 John Dowling, 'Fianna Fáil to promise every citizen €188 every week', *Irish Independent*, 28 December 2015 (http://www.independent.ie/irish-news/politics/fianna-fil-to-promise-every-citizen-188-every-week-34317330.html).

35 Willie O'Dea, 'Basic incomes for all would end the welfare poverty trap and give people greater control of their lives', *Irish Independent*, 19 January 2017.

36 Ibid.

has not done any costing on this proposal.

Dr Seán Healy of Social Justice Ireland presented a paper to the BIEN (Basic Income Earth Network) International Congress of 2012. Entitled 'Why and How in Difficult Times: Financing a UBI in Ireland', the paper's context was the economic crisis that had engulfed Ireland and the EU as a result of the economic collapse in 2008.[37] Healy claimed that a number of decisions made seriously damaged the situation of Ireland's most vulnerable people, and the infrastructure on which they depend.[38] Nevertheless, he argued that a 'basic income is affordable, feasible and politically viable in Ireland today. It is an essential component of any sustainable, equitable and inclusive future for present and future generations in Ireland. It is clear, simple, transparent and easy to administer, unlike the current tax and welfare system.'[39]

Healy supports UBI because of Social Justice Ireland's commitment to equity and social justice. He argues that UBI would narrow the gap between rich and poor, treat men and women equally and, from a bureaucratic perspective, would make the whole process of supporting people much simpler. He estimated that the scheme could be paid for by a Social Responsibility Tax, payable by employers. This tax would replace Employers' PRSI which, currently, amounts to 8 per cent of the employee payroll. The scheme would also require an income tax rate of 45 per cent on all personal income. This 45 per cent would replace income tax, PRSI and the Universal Social Charge (USC).[40]

In November 2020, the Irish government's arts and culture recovery taskforce requested that actors, musicians and artists receive a universal basic income because their income has plummeted during the pandemic.[41]

37 Seán Ward, op. cit., 86.
38 Ibid.
39 Ibid.
40 Ibid.
41 Colm Keena and Jennifer Bray, 'Cabinet to discuss basic income scheme for arts and culture sector', *The Irish Times*, 16 November 2020.

UBI for Britain

In Britain, Gordon MacIntyre-Kemp, Chief Executive of Business Scotland, supports UBI. He estimates that the provision of UBI for Britain would cost £300 billion if every adult received £6,000 per year. He argues that if all other welfare and state pensions were placed in this pot, it would cost £70 billion more than at present to fund UBI for all of Britain. There would be major savings in the area of poverty reduction and also in the health services, because of the improvement in people's health. People would be much more secure and content because they would be making choices for themselves, rather than having those choices made by faceless bureaucrats. MacIntyre-Kemp and many proponents of UBI are adamant that it is a political choice that societies need to make, and, therefore, it is not primarily a technical or financial issue. That is why it is so important to discuss it in detail, and to set up and thoroughly research pilot projects in different parts of the UK.

Many anti-poverty lobby groups favour UBI. They believe that it will create a fairer, less complex system than the current mix of welfare and other benefits. The former leader of the Labour Party, Jeremy Corbyn, has said that he, and the Shadow Chancellor, John McDonnell, were considering putting the policy in the party's next manifesto.[42] In a speech in London, in September 2016, Jeremy Corbyn spoke about the possibility of introducing UBI to Britain as the best way to protect workers against the insecurity of today's labour market. Corbyn was also clear that recent technological changes and the gig economy will mean increased pressure on working households during the next few years.[43]

Unions in Britain, such as the Trade Union Congress (TUC), the British Trade Union (GMB) and Unite, support UBI. Becca

42 Rachel Roberts, 'Scotland set to pilot universal basic income scheme in Fife and Glasgow', *The Independent*, 2 January 2017 (http://www.independent.co.uk/news/uk/home-news/scotland-pilot-universal-basic-income-ubi-snp-fife-and-glasgow-scheme-a7505411.html).

43 Shehab Khan, 'Jeremy Corbyn pledges Labour party will investigate idea of universal basic income', *The Independent*, 17 September 2016 (http://www.independent.co.uk/news/uk/politics/jeremy-corbyn-pledges-labour-party-universal-basic-income-a7313266.html).

Kirkpatrick is a community organiser and chairperson of Unison's West Midlands community branch. She told Sonia Sodha, a columnist working with *The Guardian*, that her own experience of insecurity has meant that she can empathise with people and groups across society who feel abandoned by government policies that do not address their needs. She gives the example that, if she had a basic income, she could invest a lot more of her time in supporting her younger sister who is disabled.[44]

UBI for Scotland

In Scotland interest in UBI has been growing in recent years. At their conference in March 2016, the Scottish Nationalist Party (SNP) passed a motion supporting the introduction of UBI to replace the current welfare system.[45] The SNP believes that UBI can, potentially, provide the foundations that will eliminate poverty, make work pay and ensure that all citizens can live with dignity.

Matt Kerr, a Labour Party councillor in Glasgow, has backed the introduction of UBI in Scotland because, in his experience, it is the best way to tackle poverty. In 2017, the Labour Party, which combines Glasgow and Fife councils, were already designing trials for UBI. Under UBI, welfare benefits such as Jobseekers' Allowance, working tax credits and state pensions would be replaced by a single, unconditional flat-rate payment, regardless of whether the recipient was in paid employment or not. Any money earned above this would be subject to taxation. Matt Kerr claims that it was his investigations into poverty that convinced him that a basic income was the right step forward.[46] He points out that one third of children in Glasgow live in poverty, which is an extraordinary indictment of

44 Sonia Sodha, 'Is Finland's basic income a solution to automation, fewer jobs and lower wages?' *The Guardian*, 27 February 2017 (https://senscot.net/is-finlands-basic-universal-income-a-solution-to-automation-fewer-jobs-and-lower-wages-2).

45 Ibid.

46 'Universal basic income trials being considered in Scotland', *The Guardian*, 1 January 2017 (https://www.theguardian.com/politics/2017/jan/01/universal-basic-income-trials-being-considered-in-scotland).

government policies. Kerr sees UBI as a way of simplifying Britain's labyrinthine welfare system, but it is also about promoting solidarity across society. Such policies would show that everyone is valued and that the government has an obligation to support people financially. He is convinced that a UBI introduction would make for a better and more mature relationship between the individual and the state.[47] Kerr is clear that much more study needs to be done through pilot projects, to ensure that the form of UBI that will be introduced will fit the particular circumstances of Scotland, especially in cities such as Glasgow.[48]

Economist Guy Standing believes that there is no reason why a city or a country could not afford to have a basic income for everybody. He points out that in Britain, tax reliefs for the wealthy and corporations come to about £400 billion a year. This alone could be used to pay for a basic income for everybody.[49]

A UBI Project in Canada

One of the first experiments with UBI took place in 1974 in the town of Dauphin in north-west Winnipeg, Canada. Everyone received a basic income for a period of four years. After that, a conservative government was elected, and it decided to terminate the programme. There was no analysis of the effectiveness of the initiative. All the data collected was packed into 2,000 boxes and stored in the attic of a warehouse. It lay there unused for thirty years, until Evelyn Forget, Professor of Economics at the University of Manitoba, discovered it in 2009.

For three years she subjected the data to numerous statistical analyses. These analyses showed that there were multiple benefits from UBI. The people became richer, smarter and healthier. School attendance increased and hospitalisation decreased by 8.5 per cent.

47 Ibid.
48 Ibid.
49 Matthew Keegan, 'Benefit or burden? The cities trying out universal basic income', *The Guardian*, 27 June 2018 (https://www.theguardian.com/cities/2018/jun/27/benefit-or-burden-the-cities-trying-out-universal-basic-income).

The fear of conservatives that people would down tools and stop working was not realised. The only people who worked less were young mothers and students who stayed longer at school.[50]

It comes as a surprise that in a developed country like Canada nearly one in five children lives in poverty. In fact, this is one of the highest rates of childhood poverty in the membership of the Organisation for Economic Cooperation and Development (OECD), and three times more than the Nordic nations of Northern Europe. For this reason, leaders from across the political spectrum have supported the idea of UBI in Canada.[51] A new government for the province of Ontario was elected on 21 August 2018, with Doug Ford as premier. He had promised to lower gas prices and slash government spending.[52] Nevertheless, during the 2018 election campaign, Ford promised to allow the three-year basic pilot programme to run its course.

Two months after being elected, Ford's Conservative government decided to abandon the basic income pilot project of the previous Liberal government. The pilot project had recruited 4,000 participants across three regions of the province. It had a budget of $150 million. The people who benefitted from the project ranged from those in low-paying or precarious jobs to those on social assistance.[53] After Ontario had launched its pilot scheme, recipients began to detail how it had changed their lives. Many said that they could now afford healthier food and warm clothes for winter weather. One person stated that he felt he could afford to visit his dentist for the first time in years. Others had returned to education or invested in their own companies. The Conservative Party criticised the pilot project as expensive and unsustainable. In 2018, when Lisa MacLeod, the Ontario minister responsible for

50 Rutger Bregman, 'The easy way to eradicate poverty', *The Guardian*, 6 March 2017.
51 Ashifa Kassam, 'Ontario's new Conservative government to end basic income experiment', *The Guardian*, 1 August 2018 (https://www.theguardian.com/world/2018/aug/01/ontarios-new-conservative-government-to-end-basic-income-experiment).
52 Ibid.
53 Ibid.

social services, announced the end of the UBI pilot project, she did admit that the new government had backtracked on its campaign promise to keep the province's basic income pilot project in place. She blamed the situation faced by the Progressive Conservatives on taking office.[54]

Taxing Companies to pay for UBI

In the US, the state of Alaska has, since 1976, paid a yearly dividend from oil revenue of between $1,000 and $2,000 to each person in the state. Since everyone, including children, is entitled to the money, this can be a significant financial support for some families. In February 2017, Indian economist Kaushik Basu, a former chief economist with the World Bank, wrote an article for *Project Syndicate* recommending that the US consider some form of universal basic income 'as a partial solution to the economic insecurity of the working class'.[55]

During the mid-term elections in the US in 2018, 60 per cent of voters backed the passing of San Francisco's Proposition C. This initiative was designed to tax firms with an annual turnover of more than $50 million in order to generate $300 million to address poverty and homelessness in the area. Marc Benioff, the founder and CEO of software company Salesforce, supported this plan. He contributed $8 million to get the proposal on the statute books. Regrettably, the tax was opposed by many of the high-tech companies, such as Twitter, and the online payment service, Stripe. Those who supported this tax make the point that property prices have risen sharply since big tech companies moved into San Francisco.

Similar schemes are being discussed in other countries. In his 2019 budget, the then British Chancellor Philip Hammond

54 Ibid.

55 Kate McFarland, 'Former Chief Economist of the World Bank: Time has come to consider some form of basic income in the US', *Project Syndicate*, 19 February 2017 (http://basicincome.org/news/2017/02/16539/).

proposed a 2 per cent tax on companies with more than £500 million in income. It is estimated that this would bring in a paltry £30 million. The French president, Emmanuel Macron, is backing a similar move with the EU in Brussels to tax tech companies, but Denmark, Sweden and Ireland are opposed to it. The reality is that high-tech companies pay little in taxes. Financial services company Standard & Poor's estimates that in the period between 2007 and 2017, the average effective rate of tax paid in the US by the country's 500 highest-valued firms was 27 per cent. However, high tech companies did not even pay that amount. For example, Apple paid 17 per cent of its US profits in tax, Alphabet (the parent company of Google) paid 16 per cent, Amazon, with US profits of more than $5.6 billion, paid 13 per cent, and Facebook paid a mere 3.8 per cent.[56]

In the context of this book, it is important to remember that it is the high-tech companies that are driving the automation revolution and benefiting from it. As the number of jobs diminishes, there will be no income tax collected from those who are unemployed. Increased automation will make the present tax system unworkable.

Conclusion

There will not be a viable future if high-tech firms continue to avoid paying their just amount of taxes. What is needed is a unitary tax, where companies would be obliged to give the tax authorities of any country in which they operate both a set of accounts from their global activities, and information, also, about their physical assets, workforce, sales and profits for the territory in question. Tax would then be decided using a formula based on these combined factors.[57] Many who consider UBI a radical move are failing to recognise that we are living in a time of unprecedented change. Tweaking our economy here and there will not deliver the changes that will be necessary, if a

56 John Harris, 'Without a tax on tech, it's the end of the state as we know it', *The Guardian*, 12 November 2018.

57 Ibid.

significant percentage of people cannot find paid work.

One of the most interesting speakers at the World Economic Forum in Davos, Switzerland, in January 2019, was Dutch historian and journalist Rutger Bregman. He used his speaking time to challenge the audience for failing to talk about taxes. His book, *Utopia for Realists*,[58] is a passionate argument for UBI, open borders, and a fifteen-hour working week, all of which he deems to be important and achievable goals.[59] This may sound utopian to many people today, but Bergman points out that many of the milestones of the last two centuries, such as ending slavery, setting up democracies and giving equal rights to women, were utopian ideas when they were first articulated.

If the new technologies currently being developed lead to widespread unemployment, and, if some sharing mechanism such as UBI is not introduced, societies around the world can begin to prepare themselves for massive struggles and, possibly, violence. On the one hand, a small elite will develop and control these new technologies, which will perform the work that humans used to do in the past. On the other hand, almost half the population will not have work and will be forced to eke out a living while struggling to meet their basic needs. Unless equitable solutions are found, there will be serious anger against the elite, and a constant threat of violence of the kind that was seen in Paris in 2018 and 2019. This is not the kind of stable society that would generate the peace and harmony to which we all aspire. In the context of these new technologies, all sectors in a country must strive to build a better and more equitable society.

58 Rutger Bregman, *Utopia for Realists*, New York, NY: Back Bay Books/Little, Brown and Company, 2016.

59 'Meet the folk hero of Davos: the writer who told the rich to stop dodging taxes', *New Scientist*, 31 January 2019 (https://www.vox.com/future-perfect/2019/1/30/18203911/davos-rutger-bregman-historian-taxes-philanthropy).

Chapter 11
Catholic Social Teaching and Work

Major social problems in developed countries, such as drug abuse and violence, can be exacerbated by unemployment, especially when it reaches 15 per cent or more. Throughout this book, I have argued that because of AI and the increasing use of robots and drones, a significantly greater number of people will be unemployed. Consequently, they will have no access to an income. Will people begin to demand a basic income, as I have argued?

Catholic Social Teaching

One of the key elements of Catholic Social Teaching is that work is an important activity for human beings. In most economic and political systems, work is seen as a commodity, something one does in exchange for something else, such as an income. However, in Catholic Social Teaching, work is seen, not as a commodity, but as crucial and central to an individual's self-worth. It also contributes to the development of one's self, family, community and the larger society.[1] In *Laborem Exercens* (On Human Work), Pope John Paul II expanded on this understanding of work, stating that 'work is an obligation, that is to say, a duty on the part of everyone; everyone must work both because the creator has commanded it, and because of his/her own humanity which requires work in order to be maintained and developed' (*LE*, 17, 18). In *Laudato Si'* (On Care for Our Common Home) Pope Francis writes that 'we are created with a vocation to work' (*LS*, 128). He goes further, saying that 'developing the created world in a prudent way is the best way of caring for it, as this means that we ourselves become the

1 Sean Healy and Brigid Reynolds, 'Work for All: Why and How in a World of Rapid Change', A Seminar on Work as Key to the Social Question,' 13 September 2001 (unpublished paper).

best instrument used by God to bring out the potential which he himself inscribed in things' (*LS*, 124). We are called to 'till and to keep' the garden of the world (Genesis 2:15), to collaborate, through our work, with the Son of God for the redemption of humanity (*LE*, 27).

Work is the key to authentic social development. In *Centesimus Annus* (31) (1991) Pope John Paul II writes that '*work is with others and work is for others and that the fruit of this labour* offers occasions for exchange, relationship and encounter.'[2] Work cannot therefore be properly evaluated if its social nature is not taken into account.[3]

This communitarian dimension of work was quite central to the Irish workers who built roads, railways and houses in Britain and the US over the last two centuries. These migrant workers often worked with relatives who had already settled in these countries during the previous decades, or with people from their home town or county. Both of these groups looked out for the welfare of the new workers and helped them in many ways.

In the preface to *Laborem Exercens*, Pope John Paul II insisted that 'work is something particularly human, done in a community of persons, a condition which marks and, in a sense, constitutes the very nature of work'. I wonder what the experience of construction workers or any other workers will be, if they are cut off from contact with colleagues and surrounded instead with smart machinery. Will it lead to an increase in mental health issues and alienation?

Pope Francis is clear that replacing humans with machines is not a good thing. In *Laudato Si'* he states that 'the goal should not be that technological progress increasingly replaces human work, for this would be detrimental to humanity' (*LS*, 128). He recognises that 'the orientation of the economy has favoured a technological progress in which the cost of production is reduced by laying off workers and replacing them with machines. This is just another way

2 *Compendium of the Social Doctrine of the Church*, Dublin: Veritas Publications, 2004.
3 Ibid.

in which we can end up working against ourselves. The loss of jobs also has a negative impact on the economy through the progressive erosion of social capital; the network of relationships of trust, dependability, and respect for rules, all of which are indispensable for any form of civil existence' (*LS*, 128).

In Catholic Church teaching and that of most religions, there is very little reflection on how robots will affect human employment. In the encyclical *Laudato Si'*, Pope Francis criticises 'the economy [which] accepts every advance in technology with a view to profit, without concern for its potentially negative impact on human beings. Finance overwhelms the real economy. This happens because groups whose only interest is in maximising profits have no concern for the environment and the rights of future generations' (*LS*, 109). Pope Francis is adamant that people must have access to work, not just for the financial benefits it brings them, but because of its impact on culture and spirituality. He writes, 'work is a necessary part of the meaning of life on this earth, a path to growth, human development and personal fulfilment' (*LS*, 128).

In an article in *The New York Times* in December 2016 Claire Milller reflected on how new technologies have allowed a steel company in California to slim down its workforce by 75 per cent, yet keep production at the same level.[4] In the article, Miller interviewed fifty-six-year-old Sherry Johnson. Her first job was at a local newspaper, where one of her tasks was to feed paper into the printing machine of the newspaper. When her employers bought an automated machine to do this work, her job simply disappeared. She explained her frustrations to Miller. 'It actually kind of ticked me off because it's like, how are we going to make a living?'[5] Her next move was to study computer science, but that was a little too late. 'The twenty- and thirty-year-olds are more up to date on

4 Claire Cain Miller, 'The Long-Term Job Killer is Not China', *The New York Times*, 21 December 2016 (https://www.nytimes.com/2016/12/21/upshot/the-long-term-jobs-killer-is-not-china-its-automation.html).

5 Ibid.

that stuff than we are because we did not have that when we were growing up.'[6] Ms Johnson is now on disability benefit and lives in a social housing scheme in Jefferson City, Tennessee.[7] Will similar scenarios be played out across different cultures, as robots, drones and algorithms take more and more jobs? How will society cope with the chaos that this will cause? During the Covid-19 pandemic, we got an insight into how people might react to being out of work. After a few weeks of cocooning, some people gathered together in various states of the US, occasionally carrying arms, to demand that the economy be opened up again to allow them to go back to work. If there are jobs for only 40 or 50 per cent of the population, what will those unable to get a job do?

Even in countries where people change jobs regularly, identification with one's work is very important. In a Gallup survey in the US in 2014, 55 per cent of workers said that they got a sense of identity from their job. The figure for graduates was even higher, at 70 per cent.[8] Epidemiologists have long been aware that job satisfaction, or lack of it, can affect one's health, both physical and mental. Pressure, strain, stress and boredom in the workplace can have a damaging impact on mental health, and need to be addressed by employers and civic society. Studies on the relationship between job satisfaction and health found that those who were happy in their jobs were more likely to be healthy, and less likely to suffer from depression or anxiety or have low self-esteem.[9]

There is also mounting evidence that current trends in employment may be eroding job satisfaction. New work practices and rapid technological advances are seen to be changing the nature of many jobs. When organisations have a tight deadline, employees are often required to work longer shifts than their contracted

6 Ibid.
7 Ibid.
8 Michael Bond and Joshua Howgego, 'I work, therefore I am', *New Scientist*, 25 June 2016.
9 C. L. Cooper (ed.), *The Theories of Organisational Stress*, Oxford: Oxford University Press, 1999.

hours stipulate. As we have seen throughout this book, when work becomes more automated and inflexible, employees have less and less control over their workload. With smartphones, the employee is easily contactable and is therefore always available to the employer for work duties. Thus, a sense of job insecurity is growing in the workplace. Pope Francis teaches that work should 'be the setting for this rich personal growth, where many aspects of life enter into play: creativity, planning for the future, developing our talents, living out our values, relationship to others, and giving glory to God. It follows that, in the reality of today's global society, it is essential that we continue to prioritise the goal of access to steady employment for everyone' (*LS*, 127).

However, as we have seen throughout this book, AI, robots, drones and 3D printing are undermining the reality of steady employment for everyone. On 1 May 2020, the Feast of St Joseph the Worker, Pope Francis prayed that no one would be lacking a job and 'that all would be paid justly and may enjoy the dignity of work and the beauty of rest'.[10] Is this ambition realistic if, as a result of new technologies, only 40–50 per cent of workers will have paid employment? Perhaps this is an area where we will have to revisit and revise Catholic Social Teaching, in light of the fact that few people will have paid employment.

Working with robots is also causing physiological stress, as is clear from watching Maxim Pozdorovkin's documentary film, *The Truth About Killer Robots*. The inspiration for making the film came when Pozdorovkin heard that a manipulator robotic arm had crushed a worker to death at a Volkswagen factory in Germany. Pozdorovkin went to Germany to interview the workers. Most of them were forbidden to talk about the accident, but many of them shared their experience about the perils of automation. They maintained that

10 Pope Francis, 'May no one be without work, dignity, a just wage, prays pope,' *La Croix International* staff (with Catholic News Service), 1 May 2020, Vatican City (https://international.la-croix.com/news/may-no-one-be-without-work-dignity-a-just-wage-prays-pope/12291?utm_source=Newsl).

their work environment had been made worse by the introduction of robots.[11]

Pozdorovkin also believes that the way we interact with robots will spill over into the way we interact with humans. 'We will be ruder, more aggressive and more inconsiderate to humans.'[12] We can already see this lack of empathy in the ways in which many people communicate with each other on social media today.

As one observes the potential impact of robots taking over large segments of the economy, the most frightening aspect of this new 'robot' revolution is that it seems to be happening so suddenly, yet there is still not enough discussion about it in the media or among politicians, economists and church leaders.

The Response of the Catholic Church to Automation

Religious leaders have only recently begun to address this topic. In January 2018, the message of Pope Francis to the Davos meeting centred mainly on the challenges posed by the contemporary world, and he had a word of caution about the new technologies. He points out that AI, robotics and other technological innovations must be used in a way that contributes to the well-being of humanity and the protection of the earth, our common home.[13] The Pope lamented that the immense technological development has not been accompanied by a development in human responsibility, values and conscience.

On World Communications Day 2019, Pope Francis called attention to the importance of the internet and social media as a source of information. He went on to emphasise the risks that

11 Zach Vasquez, 'The Truth About Robots: the year's most terrifying documentary', *The Guardian*, 26 November 2018 (https:///www.theguardian.com/film/2018/Nov/26/the-truth-about-killer-robots-the-years-most-terrifying-documentary).

12 Ibid.

13 Pope Francis, 'Message of his Holiness Pope Francis for the 53rd World Communications Day', Vatican City, 24 January 2019 (http://w2.vatican.va/content/francesco/en/messages/communications/documents/papa-francesco_20190124_messaggio-comunicazioni-sociali.html).

accompany it, in terms of sharing authentic information, and the increase in cyberbullying among young people.[14] The Holy See has stated that it will establish an International Cyberbullying Prevention Programme in the Vatican to address this phenomenon. In reflecting on the use of the internet, the Pope states that it is an opportunity to promote an encounter with others, but it can also increase our self-isolation, like a web that can ensnare us.[15]

Pope Francis is particularly concerned about the impact of the internet on young people, who are the most exposed to the illusion that social media can completely satisfy them on a relationship level. He points to the dangerous phenomenon of young people becoming 'social hermits' who risk alienating themselves completely from society and developing physical and mental health conditions as a consequence. This dramatic situation reveals a serious rupture in the relational fabric of society, one that cannot be ignored.[16] Francis called on people to become more human as they move from being individuals who perceive the other as a rival, to people who recognise others as travelling companions on the road of life. Towards the end of the message, the Pope reminds Christians that the Church herself is a network of relationships woven together by eucharistic communion, where unity is based not on 'likes' or 'unlikes' but on the truth, and the 'Amen' by which each one clings to the Body of Christ and welcomes others.[17]

In January 2019, the Catholic Churches in the European Union published a significant document, *The Robotisation of Life: Ethics in View of New Challenges*. It makes the interesting point that offering an 'electronic personality' to robots collapses the boundaries between humans and machines, between the living and the inert,

14 Archbishop Eamon Martin welcomes Pope Francis's 'message on cyberbullying', *Catholic News.ie*, 28 June 2019 (https://catholicnews.ie/archbishop-eamon-martin-welcomes-pope-francis-message-on-cyberbullying).
15 Pope Francis, op. cit.
16 Ibid.
17 Robin Gomes, 'Vatican conference on robotics and artificial intelligence', *Vatican News*, 16 May 2019 (https://www.vaticannews.va/en/vatican-city/news/2019-05/vatican-conference-robotics-artificial-intelligence-pontifical-a.html).

the human and the inhuman.[18] This document is very clear that the ethical conditions that arise in the context of robotisation are relevant more generally to the relationship between science and ethics.[19] The bishops go on to make the point that what is required is a focused ethical analysis of the impact of robotisation on the individual and society. Since AI and robots will have a huge impact on our lives, it is important that Christians and people of faith must join the conversation about AI, and the integral role that ethics must play in designing these new technologies. For example, the 115-page Irish government publication, *Future Jobs Ireland 2019*, which refers to the digital economy, does not mention ethics. People of faith should insist that AI is understood as a public good in society, and its regulation should not be left to powerful digital corporations in the US and China which may not be subject to governmental or adequate regulatory processes. It is crucial that AI corporations, governments and civil society cooperate on this, to ensure that digital technology is used safely and responsibly. Religions, both nationally and globally, can play a vital role in promoting this engagement.

In February 2019, the Pontifical Academy for Life held a two-day conference on 'Robo-ethics: Humans, Machines and Health'. At a papal audience during the conference, Pope Francis said that this technology could potentially benefit all humans, but that it could also have a negative effect on society.[20] Many of those who spoke during the two-day workshop were experts in robotics and technology. The seminar presented some of the most up-to-date developments in this technology. It also gave many examples of the growing use of robots in manufacturing, medicine, surgery, elder care and the service industries.

Some of those present at the conference were experts in the social

18 The Catholic Churches in the European Union, *Robotisation of Life: Ethics in View of New Challenges*, January 2019.

19 Ibid., 2.

20 'Technology should service humanity not the reverse pope warns', *Sunday Examiner*, 3 March 2019.

sciences, philosophy and theology. Emmanuel Agius, Professor of Moral Theology and Philosophical Ethics at the University of Malta, was critical of the direction these new technologies are taking. According to him, engineers, designers and programmers tend to focus on technical challenges and advances in technology, and are slow to address the ethical issues that result from these technologies.[21] Agius is convinced that moral agency is a characteristic of humans, not machines, and no matter how intelligent the robots are, the only choices that they make are as a result of programming by human beings. Marita Carballo, president of Argentina's National Academy of Moral and Political Science, explored the impact of replacing humans with robots. She was adamant that eye-to-eye contact or a hug cannot be replaced by a robot.[22]

In his speech to the delegates, the Pope warned that technology should never be seen as a foreign and hostile force against humanity because it is a human invention – a product of human creativity.[23] As a result of this conference, the Pontifical Academy for Life dedicated its 2020 assembly to ethical considerations connected to AI.

In November 2018, the social affairs commission of COMECE, the Commission of the Bishops' Conference of the European Community, issued a report calling on politicians to assist workers in an era when technology continues to transform jobs across Europe. The bishops highlighted factors such as the blurring of boundaries that once separated professional and private life, the decreasing availability of traditional middle-class jobs and the difficulty young people have in finding permanent jobs that include health and pension benefits.[24] The bishops believe that the 'polarisation' of the

21 Liam McIntyre, 'Robotics need ethical guidelines, speakers say at Vatican meeting', *Catholic News Service*, 1 March 2019.

22 Ibid.

23 Ibid.

24 Anne Condodina, 'New policies needed to protect workers, says EU bishops' commission', *Crux*, 8 November 2018 (https://cruxnow.com/church-in-europe/2018/11/08/new-policies-needed-to-protect-workers-says-eu-bishops-commission/).

job market is growing with the disappearance of blue-collar jobs, with many jobs being relocated to countries where labour costs are cheaper, or replaced by robots or algorithms. They went on to stress that the goal is to make work accessible and sustainable for all, with an economy that is centred around the people it is meant to serve. The bishops pointed out that 'decent' work includes a safe environment, a living family wage, time off to spend with family, and that workers have a say in how their work is organised.[25] The commission also proposed that the EU recognise family work and volunteering. Family members who care for their children and the elderly 'perform a vital service for the common good', and should, therefore, 'have access to health insurance and be entitled to receive an adequate pension'. In terms of sustainability, the bishops' committee proposed that in line with the encyclical on the environment, *Laudato Si'*, the EU should become a leader in promoting occupations and enterprises that care for the environment.

Religions and the Sustainable Development Goals (SDGs)

In March 2019, I attended a conference on 'Religions and Sustainable Development' (SDGs), in the Vatican. The conference was hosted by the Dicastery for Promoting Integral Human Development and the Pontifical Council on Interreligious Dialogue. It was an extraordinary event, which should have attracted far more media coverage than it received from the secular press, since it brought together UN personnel as well as representatives of different religions from around the globe, to discuss their understanding of sustainable development in the light of the various religious traditions, including Judaism, Islam, Buddhism, Hinduism and tribal religions. The Conference was opened by the Vatican Secretary of State, Cardinal Pietro Parolin, and this emphasised the importance of the topic. He made the point that very often in discussions about sustainable development, little emphasis is given to what religions

25 Ibid.

can contribute on this topic. In the Abrahamic religions – Judaism, Christianity and Islam – life is seen as a gift from God, and every human being is made in the image and likeness of God. Reverend Swami Agnivesh, from India, spoke movingly about the plight of the bonded labourers in India who experience slave-like conditions. According to him, this plight affects the lives of tens of millions of people, even though the Indian Supreme Court has condemned the practice of bonded labour.

Mgr Robert Joseph Vitillo, Secretary General of the International Catholic Migration Commission (ICMC), spoke on the future of work. He talked about the dignity of work for both men and women. However, neither he, nor any other speakers at the conference, mentioned the fact that automation, driven by AI, algorithms, robots, drones and 3D printing, is currently reshaping the reality of work so that, in the future, 40 or 50 per cent of people in a given area may not have access to paid work.

The Catholic Church often arrives at issues a little breathless and a little late. For example, it has sometimes been slow in responding to important issues, like industrialisation and the destruction of the natural world. In nineteenth-century Britain the 'Satanic' mills of the machine-owning industrialists were destroying the lives of the poor in an extraordinary way, as was depicted in the books of Charles Dickens (1812–1870). In 1850, life expectancy in Manchester was estimated at thirty-two years, well below the national average of forty-one years. At that time, Karl Marx and Friedrich Engels were writing about how the wage earners were being enslaved by the factory owners. Yet, it was 1891 before Pope Leo XIII published *Rerum Novarum*, an encyclical that addressed some of these issues. The encyclical would have been much more effective if it had been published in 1831, when tens of thousands of young people left their rural villages to work in the factories of disease-ridden Manchester.

Likewise, the Catholic Church was late in recognising and challenging the destruction of the environment that has taken place during the last century. Many serious environmental issues were highlighted in Rachel Carson's bestselling book, *Silent Spring*, which was published in April 1962. People will agree that the Second Vatican Council, which began in 1962 and continued until 1965, brought about a great number of positive changes in the Catholic Church. Still, it had little to say about the environment. It is worthwhile asking whether, if 50 per cent of the people who voted at the Council were women, would the environment have been overlooked in such a dramatic fashion?

Conclusion

I believe that preparing for and responding to the social impacts of AI and automation will be the defining challenge of the next decade, and that the Catholic Church and all religions will need to take this issue on board, as a central pastoral focus of their work at local, national and global level. Groups focused on this topic should be formed in every parish and diocese to address this issue. Obviously, those who are working at a national level should be in touch with research groups in universities and the trade unions. In this area, the Catholic Church could work closely with other Christian Churches and all religions, because the reality of automation will affect everyone. The Vatican has a network of contacts throughout the world because its papal nuncios have ambassadorial status in many countries. These nuncios and other employees in the various apostolic nunciatures around the world could pass on information on developments in AI and robots to a coordinating group in Rome. At regular intervals, this group could publish documents, hold conferences and give guidance on how to cope with the new technologies.

In the future, most of the people dealing with this issue in the Catholic Church and in other religions will be lay people, not clergy. It would be nothing short of disastrous, if it takes the Catholic Church and other religions thirty or forty years to respond to the impact these new technologies are making and will continue to make in the world. As we enter this fourth Industrial Revolution, we have a short window of opportunity to ensure that these new technologies are aligned with the open, inclusive and dynamic world that we want for all people and for all creation. Preparing for and responding to the social, economic and religious impact of automation will be the defining challenge of the next two decades.

Afterword

The world was completely unprepared for the challenges that the Covid-19 pandemic caused globally in 2020. Looking back at the pandemic society should have been much better prepared for it because we had known that viruses and pathogens have leaped from other species to the human population. The twenty-first century has given us a host of pandemics including Covid-19, SARS, MERS, Ebola, HIV, Zika, and H1N1.

Now that humans are colonising every ecosystem, we can expect more frequent and often more deadly pandemics in the future, especially as human population[1] levels will reach ten billion within the next thirty years. Humans are changing ecosystems in ways that favour animals such as bats and rodents, which often carry diseases that will eventually affect the human population. This happened with the coronavirus in Wuhan in China towards the end of 2019. It is believed that a pangolin, a scaly, nocturnal animal, native to Africa and Asia, is the most likely candidate for carrying that virus to humans. In 2019, it is estimated that 200,000 pangolins were smuggled into China for use in traditional medicine which is one of the reasons that pangolins are now facing extinction globally. The only way we can avoid pandemics in the future is by changing our impact on the natural world, deciding to live in a more sustainable way and restoring ecosystems that have been destroyed. Yet, most

1 Covid-19 is the third coronavirus to pass from animals into humans in the last twenty years. The first of these was SARS which killed ten per cent of those who contracted it. While MERS, another coronavirus, was also quite deadly. Covid-19 is not as deadly as these other coronaviruses, but it is very infectious and, therefore, transmittable. The next pandemic might combine the infectiousness of Covid-19 with the deadly characteristics SARS or MERS.

of the discussion on Covid-19, centres on developing a cure or a vaccine, not on how we must change our behaviour towards the natural world and thus avoid pandemics in the future.

There are many similarities between the impact of Covid-19 and the changes that AI will bring to our society in the next two decades. Covid-19 has dramatically changed work practices, with many people now opting to work from their homes. This trend seems likely to continue, according to a study of 750 European employers published during the last week of September 2020. 41 per cent have plans to make it easier for staff to continue working from home once offices reopen.[2]

In terms of artificial intelligence (AI) and automation, the main change that I have focused on in this book is the fact that many people will not be able to find paid work in retailing, caring roles, agriculture and financial services – to name but a few.

I believe that, once again, if we rely purely on market forces, we will be very unprepared for the impact this will have on human society. Investing in education will be essential as people will need to reskill and upskill themselves at various times in their lives. Governments will need to subsidise adult education courses and retraining so that people will be able to make the necessary transition. That is why I think that the Catholic Church, in dialogue with other Christian Churches and other world religions, has a serious obligation to put a lot of effort and thought into researching the impact of AI on peoples' lives. Otherwise, the money of the elite and the technology of large corporations will prevail, and the lives of millions of people will be impoverished, as happened during the first Industrial Revolution in the nineteenth century.

Commentator and economist David McWilliams notes that young people, who often work in the retail, hospitality and tourist industries, have been particularly affected. Youth unemployment in

2 Pilita Clark, 'The looming legal minefield of working from home', *The Irish Times*, 28 September 2020.

Ireland in May 2020 was at a staggering 50 per cent due to Covid-19.[3] Will young people also be the group most affected by the automation technologies? We must do all in our power to ensure that this does not happen.

Is it too much to expect that those in leadership roles in society, especially politicians, academics and economists, can for once anticipate events, rather than simply responding to them when they begin to cause problems?

3 David McWilliams, 'The programme for government largely ignores the young', *The Irish Times*, 20 June 2020.

Index

Index

Select Bibliography

Chivers, Tom, 'The AI Does Not Hate You', in *Superintelligence, Rationality And the Race To Save The World*, London: Weidenfeld and Nicolson, 2019.

Dunlop, Tim, *Why the future is Workless*, NSW: NewSouth, 2016

Ford, Martin ,*The Rise of the Robots, Technology and the Threat of Mass Unemployment*, London: Oneworld, 2016.

Harari, Yuval Noah, *Homo Deus, A Brief History of Tomorrow*, London: Vintage, 2015.

New Scientist Instant Expert, *Machines that Think: Everything you need to know about the coming age of artificial intelligence*, London: John Murray Learning, 2017.

Ross, Alec , *The Industries of the Future*, London: Simon and Schuster, 2016.

egmark, Max, *Life 3.0: Being Human in the Age of Artificial Intelligence*, ndon: Penguin Books, 2017.

off, Shoshana, *The Age of Surveillance Capitalism, The Fight for a Human e at the New Frontier of Power*, London: Profile Books, 2019.